This book may be kept
Twenty-one days
A fine of $0.20 per day will
be charged for each day it is overdue

D0933683

ARTHURIAN ROMANCE

ARTHURIAN ROMANCE

Seven Essays

EDITED BY

D. D. R. OWEN

SCOTTISH ACADEMIC PRESS

EDINBURGH & LONDON

1973

Reprinted from
FORUM FOR MODERN LANGUAGE STUDIES
Volume VI No. 1

———

Published by
Scottish Academic Press Ltd.
25 Perth Street, Edinburgh 3

Distributed by
Chatto and Windus Ltd.
40 William IV Street
London WC2

ISBN 0 7011 1662 5

This edition first published 1970
Reprinted 1972
Reprinted 1973

Deduced in EGLE

Printed in Great Britain by
Lewis Reprints Ltd.
member of Brown Knight & Truscott Group
London and Tonbridge.

FOREWORD

There is probably no area in medieval studies that merits, or indeed currently receives, more attention than Arthurian romance. The present collection of essays reflects not only this general interest in the subject, but also some of the more important lines of enquiry at present being pursued. There is close textual scrutiny beside the more general view of artistic purposes and postures, comment on certain attitudes of modern scholarship as well as on those of the medieval poets, discussion of works either as self-sufficient creations or in their relationship to other texts or traditions. The authors of the essays were given no brief, and their approaches range from the strictly factual to the expression of more or less provocative opinion (a number of the contributions have been read and discussed as papers in various gatherings) ; but it is hoped that all will prove useful and stimulating to those who take an interest in the rich field of medieval literature.

Perhaps the days are far past when the finest literary creations of the Middle Ages were regarded as gauche products of serious but fundamentally naïve men. Nowadays we may sometimes risk going to the other extreme by reading into them too much of the complexity and insecurity of twentieth-century thought. But at least we are coming more and more to realise the possibility of the writers' critical detachment from their engagingly preposterous fictions, to realise that neither is irony a latter-day prerogative, nor is a subtle sense of humour exclusive to ourselves. So it is no accident that several of these essays probe for ironic allusion and veiled comment. At the same time, modern scholarship must keep its own methods under strict review and, as other studies here remind us, not neglect in its search for new interpretations such vital matters as artistic form, literary relationships and relative chronology ; for an interpretation that flies in the face of what is historically verifiable is perforce anachronistic, whatever other merits it may have.

The reader will find in these pages, then, facts which he may be glad to have by him, opinions with which he may or may not agree ; but most important, they will invite him to use his critical judgment on a variety of related topics and derive some enjoyment from their consideration.

D.D.R.O.

CONTRIBUTORS

TONY HUNT teaches in the French Department of the University of St Andrews and is currently preparing a study of Chrétien's *Yvain* and its foreign adaptations made in the Middle Ages.

A. H. DIVERRES is Carnegie Professor of French in the University of Aberdeen and Vice-President of the British Branch of the International Arthurian Society. He is the author of essays on Froissart's *Meliador* and has studies of Chrétien de Troyes in preparation.

D. D. R. OWEN is Senior Lecturer in French in the University of St Andrews. His publications include articles on Arthurian romance and a longer study, *The Development of the Grail Legend* (1968). He is at present collaborating on an edition of *Le Chevalier à l'épée* and *La Mule sans frein*.

D. H. GREEN is Professor of Modern Languages in the University of Cambridge. Having published major works on the earlier medieval period (*The Carolingian Lord*, 1965 ; *The Millstätter Exodus*, 1966), he has more recently turned his attention to Arthurian romance and has several forthcoming studies in this field.

W. H. JACKSON teaches in the German Department of the University of St Andrews and is preparing a monograph on Hartmann von Aue's romances stemming in part from his Cambridge Ph.D. thesis, *Love and Individualism in the German Courtly Romance* (1967).

D. S. BREWER is Fellow of Emmanuel College, Cambridge, and University Lecturer in English. His published work includes a contribution to *Essays on Malory* (ed. J. A. W. Bennett, 1963) and an edition of *The Morte Darthur*, parts 7 and 8 (1968). He is at present preparing a new edition of Chaucer's *Troilus*.

E. B. LYLE has approached Arthurian material by way of ballad studies. She has published an essay on *Thomas of Erceldoune* and, among other projects, has in preparation an edition of *Thomas the Rhymer*.

CONTENTS

I

THE RHETORICAL BACKGROUND TO THE
ARTHURIAN PROLOGUE

TRADITION AND THE OLD FRENCH VERNACULAR PROLOGUES

I. THE PROLOGUE—EARLY THEORY AND DEVELOPMENT

The origins of the prologue are to be sought in the theatre and in oratory.[1] The innovation of a prologue and set-speech preceding the parode of Greek drama is attributed to Thespis around the year 534 B.C., whilst the development of Attic oratory in the fifth century B.C. led to the collection of stock openings for forensic and political speeches.[2] Certain characteristics of the prologue as a literary genre have remained fairly constant throughout its history. In Euripides the prologue, in the form of a narrative monologue, was designed to familiarize the audience with the myth that was the subject of the tragedy and with the circumstances of the action, i.e., it was expository. The summarizing of the ensuing narrative has remained one of the functions of the literary prologue.

With Aristophanes, however, we find a new emphasis on obtaining the goodwill of the audience. The speech of Xanthias in *The Wasps* (ll. 54 ff.) contains the essence of the *captatio benevolentiae* which assumed great importance in the evolution of the prologue, especially in public oratory. In Latin this new aspect is particularly marked in Plautus, who makes liberal use of jokes to obtain the attention of his audience. The prologues of Terence are clearly apologetic. The second prologue of the *Hecyra* begins " Orator ad vos venio ornatu prologi." Elsewhere, as in *Phormio* for example, Terence resorts to the technique of attacking his detractors, a device later recommended by Cicero and beloved of the medieval poets. The *argumentum* of the play scarcely receives any attention and it is possible to regard the prologue as almost independent of the play.

Thus Greek tragedy laid the foundation of the prologue as a summary of the drama which followed and from this the literary prologue subsequently drew its function of instruction, the provision of necessary information. Latin comedy, on the other hand, increasingly gave prominence to the establishment of a relationship with the audience, a relationship which was to comprehend the quiet, the attention and the sympathy of the listeners. These two functions were retained by the prologues of late Antiquity and of the Middle Ages and gave rise to numerous *topoi* which have been studied and catalogued by Curtius, Arbusow, Lausberg and others.[3] In the hands of certain twelfth-century theoreticians these functions were also utilized, we shall see, as the basis for a formal division of the prologue into two parts, the one concerned with the audience relationship, the other forming a direct introduction to the matter of the *narratio*.

The immediate antecedent of the literary prologue, however, lies in oratory, traditionally classified as forensic, deliberative and epideictic.[4] Aristotle's treatment of the *prooemium* which is found in the *Rhetoric* Bk. III, chs. 14 and 15, preserves the dual function of the prologue as we have already observed it and provided the basis for a similar handling of it by the author of the pseudo-Ciceronian *Rhetorica ad Herennium*, by Cicero, notably in the *De inventione*, and by Quintilian in his *Institutio Oratoria*. With the Latin orators the connexion of the *exordium* to the following speech is reinforced, its practical and ornamental nature clarified.[5] The deictic reasoning (to use Aristotle's term) of the theatrical prologue made it quasi-independent of what followed it, whilst the oratorical *exordium* was thoroughly integrated in the speech and its structure by the Latin orators whose work is of great importance for medieval literary theory. These two standpoints concerning the function of the prologue play a considerable part in modern critical approaches to the interpretation of medieval works and their prologues and for this reason are emphasized here.

II. Ciceronian Rhetoric and the Prologue

The Ciceronian concept of the *exordium*[6] plays a major role in the development of the prologue and supplies the bulk of later medieval theory concerning this division of the literary work. There is considerable variety, however, in the terminology employed by writers of treatises on rhetoric to denote the opening section of a speech. In practice the *prologus* and the *exordium* soon fell together and already in Aristotle's *Rhetoric* the two terms are used almost synonymously. In accordance with the *Rhetorica ad Herennium* and *De inventione* which favour *exordium*, this is the term which will be generally used in this paper. The terms *exordium, prooemium, principium,* etc., are frequently interchangeable and any special, distinctive usage in our references will be duly noted.

The classic formulation of the function of the *exordium* is that given by Cicero in the *De inv.* I, xv, 20 :

> Exordium est oratio animum auditoris idonee comparans ad reliquam dictionem ; quod eveniet si eum benivolum, attentum, docilem confecerit.

This formula recurs in almost every important treatise on rhetoric from Cicero to the theoreticians of the later Middle Ages,[7] and is clearly illustrated by the humility formulae, sententiae, requests for silence, etc., which characterize many medieval vernacular prologues. Thus, the prologue of the fifteenth-century romance, the *Chevalier au Cygne*, offers a striking counterpart to the Ciceronian definition :

> Ceste canchon ne veut noise, ne bruit, ne tence,
> Mais douçour et escout et pais et reverence.

> (ed. C. Hippeau, ll. 4-5)

In this normal type of *exordium* or *principium* the audience is approached clearly and directly—" perspicue et protinus " (*De inv.* I, xv, 20). The Ciceronian corpus of rhetorical theory specifies in detail the methods by which the orator is to obtain the conditions of *benevolentia*, *docilitas* and *attentio* in his audience. These may now be analysed. At the same time, it will be convenient to demonstrate the parallels to be found in Old French literature as a rough indication of the trend of this paper, although our study of the transmission of classical rhetoric and its assimilation by medieval writers is yet to come.

The *benevolentia* of the audience may be obtained in four ways : *ab nostra*, *ab adversariorum*, *ab iudicum persona* (*Ad Her.* = *ab auditorum persona*), *a causa* (*De inv.* I, xvi, 22 ; *Ad Her.* I, iv, 8 ; cf. *Quint.*, IV, i, 6). The same methods are still recommended in the thirteenth century by, for example, Conrad of Mure in his *Summa de arte prosandi* (ed. Rockinger I, p. 466).

The *ab nostra* method involves the presentation of the speaker/author who may praise himself but without arrogance. Frequently he may make protestations of unworthiness, lack of ability and so on, in various humility formulae, the most general of which is the widespread *topos* of *sermo rusticus*.[8] The *ab nostra* method is exemplified in *Ille et Galeron*, Ms. P (ed. Cowper), ll. 23 ff., *Cligés* (ed. Foerster), ll. 1 ff., *Florimont* (ed. Hilka), ll. 8 ff., *La Manekine* (ed. Suchier), ll. 1 ff. and ll. 30 ff., *Ipomedon* (ed. Kölbing and Koschwitz), ll. 33 ff., *Méraugis* (ed. Friedwagner), ll. 17 ff., and cf. the *titulus* of Hartmann von Aue's *Der arme Heinrich* and *Iwein*.

The *ab adversariorum* approach involves the denigration of rivals, opponents and detractors. In Old French literature this usually takes the form of expressed contempt for the *jongleurs* and *vilains conteurs* as in *Le Couronnement de Louis* (ed. Langlois), ll. 4-5, *Erec* (ed. Foerster), ll. 20 ff., *Méraugis* (ed. Friedwagner), ll. 10 ff., *Aiol* (ed. Normand and Raynaud), ll. 7-9.

4

The *ab iudicum/auditorum persona* method finds its equivalent in references to a patron in Old French. The work may be dedicated to a patron, to his honour and worth (*Perceval, Eracle*) or the patron may have instructed the writer in his choice of subject (*Charrete*).[9]

The *a causa* technique most often consists of praise of the case or of persons involved in the case as in *Le Charroi de Nîmes* (ed. Perrier), l. 4 (praise of the hero), *La Mort Aymeri de Narbonne* (ed. du Parc), l. 3, *Le Chevalier au Cygne* (ed. Hippeau), l. 2 (" s'oiiés bonne canchon de moult grand sapience ") and ll. 33-34 (" Segnour, oiiés canchon qui moult fait à loer ").

There is a still greater variety of methods for obtaining the *attentio* of the audience (*De inv.* I, xvi, 23 ; *Ad Her.* I, iv, 7 : *Quint.* IV, i, 34). They are echoed by medieval writers on many occasions as, for example, when Alberic of Monte Cassino declares, " Attentum ergo lectorem reddere si volueris vera, honesta, utilia pollicearis " (*Flores rhetorici*, ed. Inguanez and Willard, p. 36) and many of them are easily illustrated from vernacular prologues. There is the promise of brevity in *Ipomedon* (ed. Kölbing and Koschwitz), ll. 30 ff. and ll. 42 ff., and *Amadas et Ydoine* (ed. Reinhard), ll. 23 ff. There is the promise that what is said concerns the interests of humanity or, more specifically, the interests of the audience. In Old French this method results in references to the *senefiance* of the work, in the assurance that the audience may *bien aprandre* from the *essample* or that they will receive the blessing of God if they attend closely ; see *Ille et Galeron* Ms. P (ed. Cowper), ll. 25 ff., *Amis et Amiles* (ed. Hofmann), ll. 1 ff., *Aymeri de Narbonne* (ed. Demaison), l. 2, *Guillaume de Palerne* (ed. Michelant), ll. 9-10, *Florence de Rome* (ed. Wallensköld), ll. 1 ff. The call to attention —the *audite-topos*—is too common to require illustration. *Yvain* (ll. 149 ff.) and *La Manekine* (ll. 25 ff.) contain digressions on the importance of " de cuer antandre ", as does *Jaufré* (ed. Brunel), ll. 17 ff. Attention might also be gained by showing that matters to be discussed or related concern " aliquos illustres homines " (*De inv.* I, xvii, 23), the obvious candidates in Old French being Arthur and Charlemagne. The manuals on rhetoric tell us that the creation of *voluptas* by an epideictic description is a useful way to open and to secure the audience's attention. In Old French the most commonly used device of this category, apart from sumptuous descriptions of festivities, was the stock description of Spring, the season which Priscian had recommended for descriptions in the *Praeexercitamina* (ed. Halm, X, " de Descriptione "). Such descriptions occur in *Partonopeus de Blois* (ed. Crapelet), ll. 13 ff., *Les Narbonnais* (ed. Suchier), ll. 1 ff., *Berte aus grans piés* (ed. Henry), ll. 1 ff., *Brun de la Montaigne* (ed Meyer), ll. 26 ff.[10] Finally, it is interesting to observe how medieval writers reversed one of the *topoi* for gaining attention, recommended in the Ciceronian rhetoric. It has often been pointed out that a *topos* of medieval literature is " I bring nothing new ", whereas in Antiquity it had been the opposite (cf. *Ad Her.* I, iv, 7).[11] Whether this change is due to the influence of Christian *humilitas* or not[12] it remains true of the Middle Ages that "In dieser Welt ist Originalität kein Ruhmestitel, Plagiat kein Tadel."[13] The two view-points are illustrated by the prologue to *La Mule sans frain*: "Mains sont prisiees orendroit / les viez voies que les novelles, / por ce qu'en les tient a plus beles. / Et si sont miaudres par samblant, / mes il avient assez sovent / que les viez en sont les plus chieres. / Por ce dist Paiens de Maisieres / qu'en se doit tenir totes voies / plus as viès qu'as noveles voies " (ed. Orlowski, ll. 8-16).

More briefly, *docilitas* is best obtained by a summary of the case (*Ad Her.* I, iv, 7; *Quint* IV, i, 34-35), which is supplied in *La Chançun de Willame* (ed. Tyler), ll. 1 ff., *Le Moniage Guillaume* (ed. Cloetta), ll. 1 ff., *Orson de Beauvais* (ed. Paris), ll. 1 ff., *Brun de la Montaigne* (ed. Meyer), ll. 11 ff. Alberic of Monte Cassino is echoing *De inv.* I, xvi, 23 when he recommends *brevitas* for this purpose (ed. cit., p. 37).

The material which may be introduced into the *exordium* is discussed by Quintilian (IV, i, 30-31). Sometimes matter may be introduced which is not immediately or directly concerned with the case, yet not entirely unrelated to it. This comprises *adiuncta causis*—references to time, place, public opinion, etc.—and *adiuncta personis*,[14] which may include persons connected with the characters involved in the case. As we shall see later, these *adiuncta* appear in Old French prologues as stock characters and situations.

The normal *exordium*, discussed above, one should emphasize, is essentially a *captatio benevolentiae* which might also include a rough guide to the contents of the following *narratio*. It was labelled *principium* by Cicero and Quintilian in contradistinction to a second type of *exordium* called *insinuatio*.[15] Whereas the *principium* is plain, clear and direct, the *insinuatio* approaches the audience indirectly, stealing upon them unobtrusively (*De inv.* I, xv, 20); a round-about method is used so that "insinuatio surrepat animis " (*Quint.* IV, i, 42). The *insinuatio* is used whenever the audience is unreceptive or hostile. It is employed if we are dealing with a scandalous case (*genus turpe*), if the audience is already convinced by another speaker of different views from our own, or if the audience is tired (*De inv.* I, xvii, 23; *Ad Her.* I, vi, 9; *Quint.* IV, i, 48)—tired, that is, from listening to previous speakers, "cum defessus est eos audiendo qui ante dixerunt " (*Ad. Her.* I, vi, 9). Cicero emphasizes that this last circumstance is no less common than the others, "nam ex hac quoque re non minus quam ex primis duabus in oratore nonnunquam animus auditoris offenditur " (*De inv.* I, xvii, 23). In this connexion a touch of humour, wit or such entertaining matter will be of help, for "urbanitas opportuna reficit animos" (*Quint.* IV, i, 49). The main consideration is that the case which is being dealt with should not be presented or announced to the audience directly.

The essential doctrine concerning the *exordium* which students of Cicero and Quintilian thus had available to them may be summarized as follows:

1. There are two types of *exordium*: the clear, direct approach (*principium*) and the subtle, indirect approach (*insinuatio*).

2. The principal function of the *exordium* is to secure the *benevolentia*, *attentio* and *docilitas* of the audience.

3. This aim is achieved by prescribed methods which, in late Antiquity and the Middle Ages, gave rise to numerous *topoi* or commonplaces.

4. The limits of the *exordium* should be clearly, but not abruptly marked ("ut non abrupte cadere in narrationem ; ita non obscure transcendere est optimum ", *Quint.* IV, i, 79).

5. The *exordium* is not, in every case, obligatory (*Quint.* IV, i, 72).

III. THE TRANSMISSION OF CLASSICAL RHETORIC TO THE MIDDLE AGES

So far, we have given an exposition of Ciceronian rhetorical theory, as it concerns the *exordium*, and briefly indicated some reflections of its precepts to be found in Old French vernacular prologues. In the absence of any historical study of the transmission of Ciceronian doctrine, the latter might be considered as merely fortuitous. It is now, therefore, that we turn to the problem of transmission. To what extent was the corpus of rhetorical theory, which we have examined, available to and assimilated by medieval writers ? How was it modified in transmission and adapted to the specific requirements of literary composition ? Can it be affirmed that there is a continuity of rhetorical teaching in Gaul which would render plausible the idea of a tradition of oral instruction and rhetorical education to which writers of the twelfth century would be freely exposed ? These are the questions to which we now briefly address ourselves.

The study of rhetoric in ancient Rome has been adequately covered by modern scholars.[16] In the Hellenistic age when rhetoric became also the province of the schoolmasters we already find the *auctor intellectualis* of the system which is summarized in the *Ad Herennium* and *De inventione*— Hermagoras of Temnos. In the Republican period rhetoric is definitively established in Rome, during Cicero's youth, by Philo, and in the *De inventione* Cicero himself is working with terminology which was probably already familiar. Rhetoric continued to flourish in the later Empire when the municipal schools were frequently encouraged and even supervised by the imperial government for whose increasingly centralized administration a large number of trained officials was necessary. A training in rhetoric fitted one for the higher positions of public life and it was with such an argument that Ausonius exhorted his grandson to study. With the onset of the barbarian invasions greater importance was attached to the monastic and episcopal schools which sought by practical means to preserve a literate clergy. The old view that with the collapse of the Western Roman Empire rhetorical teaching in Gaul disappeared leaving no legacy to the Frankish Kingdom can no longer be maintained. In particular, the work of Riché, Pirenne and others[17] has shown how rhetoric survived in preaching, epistolary writing, the *vitae sanctorum* and how it was preserved by the needs of state administration and by the fidelity of the senatorial families, south of the Loire, to the Roman rhetorical and cultural tradition.[18] In the ninth century we have clear evidence for the interest in Ciceronian rhetoric in the remarkable activity of Lupus of Ferrières. The *De inventione, De oratore* and the *Ad Herennium* are mentioned side by side in the celebrated letter of Lupus to Einhard, Charlemagne's biographer. We also have a similar request to Pope Benedict III for the *De oratore* and Quintilian's " *Institutiones oratoriae* " and another to Abbot Altsig of York, asking for the latter work.[19] It is clear from these letters that Lupus already possessed copies of these works or parts of them, though some copies were evidently unsatisfactory. According to C. H. Beeson, " Lupus stands at the head of medieval scholars in his knowledge of Cicero."[20] At the same time Paschasius Radbertus of Corbie knew Cicero's *De inventione* well enough to quote from it in his correspondence, and evidence of a more indirect nature can help to fill out the picture.[21] For example, for the *Rhetoric* of Alcuin we have a number of extremely well-preserved ninth-century codices and a much smaller number of manuscripts of a later date, a situation which may be explained by the fact that the direct availability of Cicero's rhetorical treatises for study at that time rendered Alcuin's excerpts of the *De inventione* superfluous, hence the good state of preservation of the early manuscripts and the small doctrinal influence exerted by him.[22] In the centuries which follow there is increasing evidence of the use of the Ciceronian treatises on rhetoric and of their availability in libraries and schools. In the tenth century Ekkehard IV of St Gall refers to Quintilian and Cicero in his *Confutatio rhetorice in facie ecclesie et sanctorum*, and it is not improbable that the monastery of St Gall possessed a *complete* copy of Quintilian.[23] The establishment of a school system, initiated by Charlemagne and subsequently recommended by his bishops in a series of councils, favoured the spread of learning and intellectual activity, promoting the teaching of the *trivium*.[24] Not only do we have the testimony of individual teachers who utilized the Ciceronian treatises, but also a quantity of medieval library catalogues which reveal copies of them in libraries all over Europe.[25] In a twelfth-century list of textbooks, christened by its editor *Sacerdos ad altare accessurus*, we find the three major rhetorical treatises mentioned side by side.[26] There is no doubt that by the twelfth century the *De inventione* and *Rhetorica ad Herennium* had long been studied and excerpted, being known as *rhetorica prima* (or *vetus* or *prior*) and *rhetorica secunda* (or *nova* or *posterior*) respectively. At this time commentaries had appeared on both ; that on *De inventione* by Thierry of Chartres[27] and one on the *Ad Herennium* by Alain de Lille.[28] In the twelfth century, too, Quintilian is excerpted in the *Rhetoric* of Ulrich von Bamberg and in an *Institutio puerorum* contained in the *Codex Zwifaltensis*. The precise nature of the influence exerted by the *Ad Herennium* on medieval writers has yet to be fully worked out, but its great importance is definitely established.[29] Although its transmission was hampered by mutilated texts, Quintilian's *Institutio Oratoria* played a considerable part in the propagation of Ciceronian rhetorical theory, as Peter of Blois acknowledges[30] and recent work has disclosed the hitherto unsuspected knowledge of it amongst many writers.[31] Of course, Ciceronian theory in medieval writers is not exclusively derived from the study of the texts of Cicero's rhetorical treatises, but also from secondhand compilations, whether they be detailed re-workings like that of Fortunatianus in the fourth century or the more encyclopaedic works of Cassiodorus, Isidore of Seville[32] and their successors, and later from excerpts contained in *florilegia*,[33] *libri manuales*[34] and the precepts of *ars dictaminis*.

IV. MEDIEVAL THEORISTS AND VERNACULAR LITERATURE

We have seen that the Ciceronian teaching with regard to the *exordium* was available to medieval students and if we consider some of the contemporary writers on rhetoric, whether their concern be with epistolary composition (*ars dictaminis* or *ars dictandi*),[35] with literary composition (*ars poetica*)[36] or with sermon composition (*ars praedicandi*)[37] we can see clearly how this teaching was reproduced.

Many of the writers in Rockinger's collection reproduce the Ciceronian formulation of the triple aim of the *exordium* (e.g. Alberic of Monte Cassino, John of Garland, Johannes Anglicus, Conrad of Mure, Conrad of Hirsau). A particularly detailed account of how *benevolentia* can be obtained is given by the anonymous *rationes dictandi* (c. 1135) (Rockinger I, 18),[38] Ugo da Bologna (ibid., I, 57), Conrad of Mure (ibid., I, 466 f.) and in the *Aurea Gemma* (Bütow op. cit., p. 68).[39] An emphasis on *humilitas* may be noted in the *rationes dictandi* and in Conrad of Mure. The terms *prologus, principium, prooemium, proverbium* are sometimes clearly defined, at other times they appear to be interchangeable and are used in an arbitrary fashion (e.g. Ludolfus of Hildesheim, Rockinger I, 367 and the Baumgartenberg Formulary, Rockinger II, 744). Cicero had classified *exordia* as being of the direct type (*principium*) or the indirect (*insinuatio*). This distinction is preserved by the twelfth-century *rationes dictandi* (Rockinger I, 19) which employ the Ciceronian terminology " protinus et perspicue " for the *principium* and " circuitio(ne) et dissimulatio(ne) " when describing the *insinuatio*.[40] Ugo da Bologna (Rockinger I, 56-57) follows Quintilian on the *transitio* in declaring that the *exordium* should not be marked off abruptly from the rest of the work and when he states that it is not always obligatory. The faults of the *exordium* as related in *De inv.* I, xviii, 26 are discussed by Conrad of Mure in his *Summa de arte prosandi* (Rockinger I, 465). The Baumgartenberg Formulary and the *Rhetorici colores* of Onulf of Speyer[41] both contain lists of sententiae whilst Bernoldus Caesariensis in the second part of his work has the rubric " Incipit secunda pars, que continet exordia seu proverbia et sentencias diversas prosayco dictamini prout dictanti placuerit inserendas " (Rockinger II, 850) in which part are included " proverbia extracta de libris Salomonis ". The recommendation of sententiae for the opening of a work is, of course, a characteristic of the twelfth and thirteenth-century manuals on poetic. Matthew of Vendôme gives many examples in his *Ars versificatoria* (Faral, pp. 113-116).[42] Similar advice is given by John of Garland (ed. Mari, pp. 905 ff.), who among his recommendations includes the employment of a *proverbium* or *exemplum* in conjunction with the *ordo artificialis*. Geoffrey of Vinsauf considers the *ordo artificialis* to be artistically superior to the *ordo naturalis* and deals with its mode of employment in detail (*Documentum* I, 1 ff., ed. Faral, pp. 266-68 ; *Poetria nova*, ll. 87 ff., ed. Faral, pp. 200-203). Teaching on the natural and artificial order of narration had already been included in the Viennese scholia on Horace's *Art of Poetry*, preserved in a codex of the tenth or eleventh century and composed by an unknown author of the Alcuin school : " omnis ordo aut naturalis aut artificialis est. Naturalis ordo est, si quis narret rem ordine quo gesta est ; artificialis ordo est, si quis non incipit a principio rei gestae, sed a medio . . .".[43] The subject is also treated by Conrad of Hirsau (Dialogus, ed. cit., p. 18) and by Bene da Firenze in his *Candelabrum*.

Thus the medieval theorists base themselves squarely on the Ciceronian model for the *exordium*. " Exordium est principium oracionis per quod ad audiendum instituitur animus auditoris " (Baumgartenberg Formulary, Rockinger II, 744 ; cf. John of Garland, ed. Mari, pp. 909 and 911). A characteristic medieval addition is the initial use of the *proverbium* or sententia, " similitudo metaphorice continens consuetudinem approbatam " (Baumgartenberg Formulary, loc. cit.) or " auctorabile dictum virtutis et moralitatis inductivum " (Conrad of Mure, Rockinger I, 467). The *exordium* or *prooemium* is " sermo preambulus ad dicenda " (Baumgartenberg Formulary), " prefacio operis " (Conrad of Hirsau), " preordinacio libri " (John of Garland)[44] and hence, essentially a *captatio benevolentiae*, with a sententia aimed primarily at securing a favourable relationship with the audience. It need have no direct connexion with the ensuing *narratio*, a point which most critics have ignored in their interpretations of the prologues to the more celebrated medieval romances.

Interestingly, however, both Conrad of Hirsau and John of Garland, having discussed this concept of what they term the *prooemium*, then proceed to examine a part of the general *exordium* which is an introduction proper to the *narratio* rather than a mere preface.

> Proemium prefacio est operis, prologus quedam ante sermonem prelocutio ; . . . Est autem omnis prologus aut apollogeticus aut commendaticius ; vel enim se excusat aut commendat . . . prologus vero comicis prosaicisque prefigitur libris et quid et quomodo vel quare scriptum vel legendum sit explicat.
> (Conrad of Hirsau : *Dialogus super auctores* ed. Huygens, ll. 124-32)

> Proemium est preordinacio libri ad instruendum, prologus est sermo inductivus subsequentis operis, sive contineat talia proemia sive non.
> (John of Garland, ed. Mari, p. 909)

From this it appears that some writers made a distinction between what are here called *prooemium* and *prologus*. The dual purpose of the prologue which we found in Antiquity here becomes the basis for a structural division of the prologue into two kinds, the first linked to what follows in a similar way to the prologue of Latin comedy (i.e. essentially a *captatio benevolentiae*) and the second (here *prologus*), resembling in function the prologue in Greek tragedy.[45] Clearly one may be too insistent in looking at medieval vernacular prologues from the latter point of view, as if their purpose were to " sum up " the matter of the *narratio*, the *auctoris intentio* and the *libri utilitas*.

The consequences of the teaching contained by these medieval manuals of rhetoric and poetic for vernacular literature of the time have been disputed, but several critics have pronounced in favour of a far-reaching and observable influence[46] and a number of stylistic studies have thoroughly borne out their conclusions.[47] Many of the doctrines were by no means new, as we have seen, when Geoffrey of Vinsauf and other authors wrote them down and must already have been known and practised.[48] A knowledge and use of these precepts by vernacular writers may, in some cases, imply a direct study of the handbooks or at least a thorough schooling in rhetoric,[49] but in other cases they suggest, rather, that such precepts and ideas were current in the literary world of the time and that, in all likelihood, they were included in oral instruction. Further evidence, with regard to prologues, is supplied by numerous studies of exordial *topoi* in medieval literature.[50]

In the 12th C. Nicolas of Clairvaux, one-time secretary to the great Saint Bernard and subsequently to the Count of Champagne, wrote to a " magistro G. archidiacono " (Gebuinus ?) of Troyes ; " Dum linguae tuae volubilitas aureo sermone diffunditur, Tullium, aut Quintillianum vel aliquem ex illis veteribus officinis perorare confiteor " (*Migne, PL* CXCVI, col. 1599).

Against the background, which we have sketched, of medieval rhetorical theory, of twelfth-century lay instruction and the schools of Troyes[51] let us investigate the rhetorical structure of the *exordium* in a work by one of Troyes' greatest vernacular writers—the *Chevalier au lion* of Chrétien de Troyes,[52] with a cautionary reminder to ourselves of the celebrated lines of Samuel Butler

> For all a Rhetoricians Rules
> Teach nothing but to name his Tools.
>
> (*Hudibras*, pt. I, c. 1, 89-90)

V. The Exordium in Arthurian Romance—Chrétien's *Yvain*

The opening section of the *Yvain* is contained by all the complete manuscripts. It is not marked off from the rest of the work, so that there is room for disagreement as to the extent of the introduction. Klose[53] considers line 39 to be an " Übergangsvers " whilst Frappier unhesitatingly refers to " Le prologue (vers 1-41) ".[54] Others have denied that there is a proper prologue at all. Kellermann states, " Der Yvain hat keinen Prolog im eigentlichen Sinn "[55] and Foerster expressed himself even more emphatically.[56] What is immediately obvious is that although the substance of the introduction is quite traditional—the setting, the post-prandial activities of the knights and their ladies, a sententia, a eulogy of Arthur—it lacks the elements of a *captatio benevolentiae* which we are accustomed to find in Old French literature of the period.[57] There is no indication of the author-audience relationship,[58] no programmatic statements *ex persona poetae*, humility formulae, requests for attention, etc. Yet it does contain traditional elements of romance prologues, as we shall see. There had, of course, been *chansons de geste* in which there was no proper prologue : thus we have the *ex abrupto* openings of the *Chanson de Roland* (though V[5] prefixes a conventional prologue), *Aliscans*, *Les Narbonnais*, *Le Pèlerinage de Charle-magne*, etc. Other works like *Renaud de Montauban* and *Le siège de Barbastre* prefix a few lines of a general character and then enter *in medias res* (cf. *Roman d'Eneas*). Léon Gautier and Rubin Halpersohn had considered the *ex abrupto* opening an indication of age but this view has been rejected by Gsteiger in a recent study.[59] None of these methods can really be exemplified in the *Yvain*. The introductory nature of the opening is suggested by the sententia ll. 31-32, the formula of l. 33, the use of the first person plural in ll. 2, 3 and 30, and the presentation of Arthur and his knights, with which the audience would be familiar as well as with the " fables " concerning him, which circulated at that time. (See Wace, *Brut*, ll. 9787 ff.). Nevertheless, we do not have in these oblique references the *principium* or direct method of opening. How, then, are we to interpret the opening of the *Yvain* ?

It will be recalled that the rhetoricians recognized a second type of *exordium*—the *insinuatio*, or indirect approach. It may be used when the audience " defessus est eos audiendo qui ante dixerunt " (*Ad Her.* I, vi, 9). Suppose that Chrétien's audience, accustomed to the recitation of romances, had wearied of hearing the conventional prologues so many times and were no longer brought to attention by this method (as the conventional operatic overture or prelude so often fails to obtain the attention of the audience). Suppose, too, that, as has been suggested in the case of the *Captivi* of Plautus,[60] there were frequent latecomers who missed part of the prologue anyway and the audience consequently took time to settle down. Chrétien hit on a new method of arousing his audience's curiosity and obtaining their attention. This was important to him, as we can see by the whole structure of the opening of the *Yvain* with its repetition of the fountain adventure (and the insertion of the herdsman's account of the fountain). There is every sign that Chrétien was particularly concerned in this work to obtain the strict attention of his audience so as to impress on them the elements of the basic décor—the fountain. He therefore chose to begin with an *insinuatio*,[61] which would steal upon the audience who, thinking that the conventional prologue had been dispensed with, would assume that the story had begun.

The work opens, not with the theme (cf. the subject of the case), the hero, or a sententia, but with the presentation of Arthur who here appears as *adiunctum personis* (cf. *Quint.* IV, i, 30-31), establishing the *tempus generale* of the story and its setting, so that, deprived of a recognizable prologue the audience is not, however, disorientated. The presentation is traditional[62] and significantly recalls the introduction of the hero or figure-head in those works which lack a prologue (e.g. *Chanson de Roland*). Placed in the *exordii initium*, its purpose is to secure a favourable response from the audience. Thus in ll. 2-3 Arthur is presented as worthy of imitation for he teaches us to be " preu et cortois ", stock epithets used similarly by Marie in *Lanval* (ll. 5-6).

The first three lines presenting the *adiunctum personis* are followed and balanced by another triad devoted to an *adiunctum causis*, the establishing of the setting. Once again, the method is purely conventional in its employ-ment of stock epithets derived ultimately from Geoffrey of Monmouth.[63] We meet the same description of setting in *Erec*, ll. 29-30, the *Charrete*, ll. 31-33 and, even more similar, in Robert Biket's *Lai du cor* (ll. 5-10 of the MS.) and then in later works like *Gille de Chyn* (ed. E. B. Place, ll. 55 f.) and the *Lai de Melion*. In each triad the *adiunctum* is presented in the first line, which is then followed by a relative clause predicating certain qualities. Hence, the common epithet " buen " (l. 1) is balanced by the equally familiar " riche " (l. 4). The repetition *proesce-preu* (*adnominatio*) is complimented by that of *coste* and *Pantecoste* (ll. 5 and 6). Furthermore, if F. W. Locke is right[64] lines 5-6 contain a pun, which he renders, " On that feast day which costs so much / which one ought to call Plentycost," where the repetition of *coste* combines with a pun on Greek παντα.[65] This would be most pertinent to Chrétien's purpose, to restore the flagging spirits of an audience perhaps (cf. *Quint.* IV, i, 49 " Urbanitas opportuna reficit animos ") and, as we have seen, a touch of humour was recommended in the *insinuatio* by *Ad Her.* (I, vi, 10) which lists as one device " ab litter-arum mutatione " which was here strictly unnecessary since the spelling *pantecoste* was a perfectly common alternative of *pentecoste*.[66]

Thus, so far, Chrétien has used two devices belonging to the *insinuatio*. He has approached his matter indirectly via *adiuncta personis et causis* (ll. 1-3 and ll. 4-6) and he has introduced humour in the form of a pun, to enliven his audience. This is the *exordii initium* which ends with the further localization of the action and a pause (l. 7).[67]

Chrétien now proceeds to an elaborate description of the activities of the knights and ladies which no doubt reflected the situation of many members of his own audience before the recitation began (cf. *Guingamor*, ll. 140 ff. ; *Le Chevalier à l' Épée*, ll. 795 ff. ; *Galeran de Bretagne*, ll. 481 1ff. ; *Durmart le Galois*, ll. 15073 ff.). Medieval audiences took great pleasure in this sort of description and it accords with the advice given by Quintilian (IV, i, 49) for the *insinuatio*. Love's " angoisses," " dolors," and " granz biens " had been a popular theme since Ovid and are found in the poems of the *vagantes* and in several early English lyrics.[68] The theme is linked here with the *topos* of *laudatio temporis acti* which, coupled with laments over aspects of the present, became a commonplace of Old French prologues.[69] The author of *Joufrois* (mid. 13th c.) seems almost to be replying to Chrétien's complaint when he says : " Ne cil ne dient mie bien / que vont disant qu'amor empire : / trop grant menchonge seivent dire, / que unques amors plus n'i vaut / qu'ele fait or, se Deus me saut ! " (ed. Streng-Renkonen, ll. 44-48). The author points out that he is talking here of true love, the love that emboldens the coward, " et de vilan fait cortois fin " (l. 35 : cf. Chrétien !) : it remains true that there are deceivers who drag love into disrepute.

It is clear that Chrétien is composing a courtly variation on a well-known exordial theme—the praise of the past (cf. *Yv.* ll. 5394 ff.). The true lovers of the past called themselves " cortois ", " preu ", " large ", " enorable ", virtues epitomized in the figure of Arthur, but deceivers of the present age do not practise what they preach (ll. 25 ff. ; cf. *Jaufré* ed. Brunel, ll. 7872-5). These lines are modelled on the commonplace denigration of *vilains conteurs* by the authors of Old French prologues[70] and bear a striking resemblance to lines in Marie's *Guigemar*,[71] on love : " Plusurs le tienent a gabeis / si cume li vilain corteis, / ki jolivent par tut le mund, / puis se vantent de ceo que funt ; / N'est pas amur, einz est folie / et mauveisté e lecherie " (ed. Lods, ll. 487-492). The same context provides the well-worn formula " fable et mançonge " (*Yv.* ll. 27 and 172 ; cf. Wace, *Brut*, ll. 9787-98) which is here adapted to the theme of love. In his *insinuatio*, then, we find Chrétien giving a courtly twist to stock epithets, familiar sayings and commonplaces drawn from earlier works, a procedure which culminates in the sententia of ll. 31-32 with its striking antithesis, subsuming the previous contrasts.[72] It seems to be a courtly adaptation of a proverb which, expressed in general military terms, occurs in the later epics.[73] The ethos of these works, however, is indicative of a much earlier period and the proverb can be illustrated from Wace : *Brut*, ll. 9165-6 : " mult valt mix morir a honor / que longes vivre a deshonor ", and from Chrétien's *Charrete* (ed. Foerster), ll. 1126 f. : " se assez miauz morir ne vuel / a enor, que a honte vivre." Thus Chrétien or another poet appears to have adapted the expression to a new outlook, not of honour, but of true love. The antithetical structure of the sententia would be already familiar to Chrétien's audience. Its function here is that of an *adiunctum causis* and the sententia appears *simpliciter* after the *ratio* (cf. Priscian, *Praeexercitamina*, ed. Halm, III), whereas it is not infrequent to find an opening sententia followed by its elaboration. The formula " por ce me plest a reconter " (*Yv.*, l. 33 ; cf. *R. de Thèbes*, l. 11 ; *Le Chevalier as deus espees*, l. 19 ; *Guillaume de Palerne*, l. 18) heralds the drawing to a close of the *insinuatio*, which ends with an *adiunctum causis* in the form of a *communis opinio* (cf. *Quint.* IV, i, 31), the Bretons' belief that Arthur's name lives on, of which we find other literary reminiscences.[74] However, the hero of the romance is not Arthur himself but one of his knights who will partake of their commander's eternal glory. " *Ramanteü* " (l. 39) thus marks the *transitio* to the *narratio* (see *Ad Her.* IV, xxvi, 35 : " transitio . . . et quid dixerit commonet, et ad reliquum con-parat auditorem "). Hence it recalls the opening (*li buens rois* / *li buen chevalier*) and prepares the audience for what is to follow.

Thus the *Yvain* opens with a *prologus* (see Conrad of Hirsau) which could be described as *commendaticius*[75] (Arthur's example) and which is in the form of an *insinuatio*. Chrétien's method is as follows. (1) He approaches his *matière* indirectly, presenting it through the use of *adiuncta*—the figure of Arthur, the court setting, the opinion on courtliness, the belief in Arthur's imperishable name. (2) He enlivens his approach by the use of humour (a pun) and by the *voluptas* afforded by a popular description (the post-prandial activities of the court). (3) He " insinuates " himself into the minds of his audience by a personal, courtly adaptation of familiar motifs, epithets and commonplaces. (4) His transition to the *narratio* is smooth so as to satisfy the recommendation "non abrupte cadere in narrationem, ita non obscure transcendere est optimum " (*Quint.* IV, i, 79). *Circuitio* was one of the most important elements of the *insinuatio*. The proof of Chrétien's success is that so many critics, doubtless reacting like his twelfth-century audience, have found a prologue wanting in the *Yvain*.

Chrétien, however, is an author who is full of surprises and woe betide the critic who thinks to have the last word ! After the altercation with Kes, Calogrenaz is enjoined (by the Queen) to commence his tale, but to his story he prefixes a little speech on the need for attention (ll. 149-174).[76] Since he had already started (ll. 59 ff.) and after an interruption was asked by the Queen to continue, such a demand from him was quite unnecessary. The emphasis on the right understanding of the tale, too, is out of place in the situation of a knight who is relating an adventure " non de s'enor, mes de sa honte " (l. 60) and which occurred seven years previously. It is clear that this digression is directed by Chrétien to his audience and it is evidence for the oral recitation of the romance. It seeks to obtain the *benevolentia* of the audience (they should not resemble those, i.e. " others ", who praise what they do not understand, ll. 149-169), and *attentio* (ll. 150, 169-70) and *docilitas* (emphasis on " de cuer antandre "—the right understanding : cf. *La Manekine*, ll. 25 ff. ; *Florimont*, ll. 5-6). The digression begins with the *audite-topos* (ll. 149-50) and includes stock affirmations like that concerning the " truth " of the story (*Yv.*, ll. 171-2 : cf. *Brut*, ll. 9787-9798, *Eracle*, l. 6200). In short, what we have here is a perfect example of a self-contained *captatio benevolentiae* aimed at securing a favourable relationship between Chrétien and his audience.[77] After the *insinuatio* which involved the audience unawares, the story proper begins and Chrétien takes a second opportunity to ensure that his audience is attentive and properly disposed. His natural desire for stylistic elegance and his primary concern with im-printing on his audience's imagination the initial scenario (the fountain) which is so crucial to the action of the whole romance[78] lead him to take the course later recommended by the manuals on poetic (see Geoffrey of Vinsauf and John of Garland) and to employ for the opening of his story, the *ordo artificialis*,[79] in this case (if we think of the fountain adventure as part one of the romance) *a medio*, for the account by Calogrenanz is situated chronologically between his experience of the fountain-adventure (seven years earlier) and Yvain's experience of it which follows. By this method the audience is made to pay close attention and the fountain topography, crucial to the romance's scenic organization, is implanted in the audience's mind.

As well as serving Chrétien's individual purpose admirably, rhetorical treatment of the *exordium* was particularly appropriate to Arthurian romance for two reasons. First, the action is set against a background of " li buens rois Artus " and his court, who are presented for the *imitatio* of the audience. Rhetoric fittingly stands at the service of eulogy. As Wallach points out,[80] Alcuin's *Rhetoric* is really a treatise on Kingship : " The *Rhetoric* is made up of rhetorical doctrine, not because Alcuin wanted to write a rhetorical textbook, but because he wished to describe the mores of Charlemagne as those that ought to serve as examples to his subjects." Second, Arthurian romances deal at length with love between persons of courtly rank. As J. M. Steadman has shown,[81] this entailed a problem of literary decorum, a principle of style. The literary treatment had to be appropriate to the subject matter and, within certain limits, *amour courtois* must inevitably exercise the poet's rhetorical technique. The problem of the three styles is treated by Geoffrey of Vinsauf (*Doc.* II, 3, 145 ff.) who continues the adaptation of style to the status of the characters depicted which we find in the Viennese scholia on Horace (ed. cit. p. 2, commentary on v. 8).

In the *Yvain* Chrétien has solved the problem of how to introduce his work, in a new and fresh manner. He has employed both species of the classical *exordium—principium* and *insinuatio*,[82] but he has further assimilated these to a medieval division of the *exordium* into *prooemium* (*captatio benevolentiae*) and *prologus* (" Sermo inductivus subsequentis operis, sive contineat [talia] proemia sive non "—John of Garland), taking the unusual step of placing the *captatio benevolentiae* second. The result is a unique exordial pattern.

> Exordium (*prologus* in form of an *insinuatio*).
> Conversation—dispute with Kes.
> Exordium (*prooemium* or *captatio benevolentiae*).
> Calogrenanz account of the fountain adventure.
> Conversation—dispute with Kes.
> Account of Yvain's fountain adventure.

A faulty introduction was a " cicatricosa facies " (*Quint.* IV, i, 61). Only a poet like Chrétien could " save his face " with such effortless expertise.[83]

St Andrews   TONY HUNT

NOTES

[1] See, for general summary, F. Stoessl, " Prologos," in *Pauly-Wissowa, Realencyclopädie der classischen Altertumswissenschaft*, Bd. XXIII, 1 (Stuttgart, 1957), sp. 632-41 and Bd. XXIII, 2 (1959), sp. 2312-2440.

[2] See G. A. Kennedy, " The Earliest Rhetorical Handbooks," *American Journal of Philology* LXXX (1959), 169-178 and id., " The Rhetoric of Advocacy in Greece and Rome," ibid., LXXXIX (1968), 419-436 ; J. Stroux, *Römische Rechtswissenschaft und Rhetorik* (Potsdam, 1949) ; C. Neumeister, *Grundsätze der forensischen Rhetorik* (München, 1964) ; E. Patrick Parks, *The Roman Rhetorical Schools as a Preparation for the Courts under the Early Empire* (Baltimore, 1945) ; M. L. Clarke, *Rhetoric at Rome* (London, 1953), p. 1 and p. 165, note 2.

[3] E. R. Curtius, *European Literature and the Latin Middle Ages*, tr. W. R. Trask, (London, 1953) ; L. Arbusow, *Colores rhetorici* (Göttingen, 1948 ; 2nd ed. rev. H. Peter, 1963) ; H. Lausberg, *Handbuch der literarischen Rhetorik*, 2 Bde (München, 1960). The *loci communes* in the prefaces of post-Ciceronian Latin authors often form the basis of the exordial *topoi* to be found in medieval writers, see T. Janson, *Latin Prose Prefaces : Studies in Literary Conventions* (Stockholm, 1964), part two.

[4] See R. Volkmann, *Die Rhetorik der Griechen und Römer*, 2te Ausg. (Leipzig, 1874), esp. pp. 89-109. On Aristotle's anomalous classification of rhetoric and its fortune in the hands of Cicero and Quintilian, who partly misunderstood it, see D. A. G. Hinks, " Tria Genera Causarum," *The Classical Quarterly* XXX (1936), 170-176.

[5] Cf. A. Porqueras Mayo, *El prólogo como género literario* (Madrid, 1957), p. 32, " Puede observarse a través de Aristoteles y Cicerón que el exordio oratorio con sus principales notas de ornato e introducción conexionada con lo que sigue—como un vestíbulo, —sin olvidar, —aunque no haya ninguna alusión directa a ello, —una difusa ' captatio benevolentiae ' menos acusada que en el teatro, es un elemento con estructura propia, capaz de aportar unos germenes llenos de potencialidad a la función introductiva."

[6] For Ciceronian rhetorical theory and its debt to earlier writers see L. Laurand, *De M. Tulli Ciceronis studiis rhetoricis* (diss. Paris, 1907) and R. Weidner, *Ciceros Verhältnis zur griechisch-römischen Schulrhetorik seiner Zeit* (diss. Erlangen, 1925) ; on its relationship to that contained in the *Ad. Her.*, D. Matthes, " Hermagoras von Temnos 1904-1955 ", *Lustrum* III (1958), 81-100 and J. Adamietz, *Ciceros de inventione und die Rhetorik ad Herennium* (diss. Marburg, 1960) ; and to that offered by Quintilian, F. Sehlmeyer, *Beziehungen zwischen Quintilians Institutiones Oratoriae und Ciceros rhetorischen Schriften* (diss. Münster, 1912). For the terminology employed consult K. M. Abbott, W. A. Oldfather, H. V. Canter et al., *Index Verborum in Ciceronis Rhetorica : necnon incerti auctoris libros ad Herennium*, (Urbana 1964). The basis of the Ciceronian definition of the *exordium* is already laid down by Anaximenes in his *Rhetoric* ed. M. Fuhrmann (Leipzig, 1966) XXIX, 1.

[7] See Fortunatianus, *Ars Rhetorica*, II, 13 (Halm I, p. 109) ; Victorinus, *Commentum in Rhetoricam Ciceronis*, I, 17 (ibid., I, p. 199) ; Martianus Capella, *De Nuptiis*, V, 545 (ed. Dick, p. 272) ; Isidore, *Etymologiae*, II, vii, 2 (ed. Lindsay) ; Alcuin, *The Rhetoric of Alcuin and Charlemagne*, ll. 473 ff. (ed. Howell, p. 96) ; Notker, *Rhetoric* (ed. H. Hattemer, *Denkmahle des Mittelalters*, Bd. III [St Gallen, 1849] p. 565) ; Anselm of Besate, *Rhetorimachia* (ed. K. Manitius, *MGH. Quellen z. Geistesgesch. d. Mittelalters*, Bd. II [Weimar, 1958] p. 117) ; William of Malmesbury *Gesta Regum Anglorum*, prologue to Bk. III (ed. Stubbs, vol. II, p. 284) ; Alberic of Monte Cassino, *Flores rhetorici* (ed. Inguanez and Willard, p. 34) ; Conrad of Hirsau, *Dialogus super auctores* (ed. Huygens, p. 16) ; Stephen of Tournai in poem ed. L. Auvray, ll. 1-4 (*Mélanges Paul Fabre* [Paris, 1902] p. 284) ; John of Garland, *Poetria* (ed. Mari, *Romanische Forschungen*, XIII [1902], p. 911) ; Alain de Lille, *Anticlaudianus*, III, 2 (*Migne, PL*, CCX col. 512) ; Buoncompagno da Signa, *Rhetorica Novissima*, IV, iii (ed. A. Gaudenzi [Bologna, 1892]) ; Dante, letter to Can Grande (c. 1319) in *Dantis Alagherii Epistolae* ed. P. Toynbee (2nd ed. Oxford, 1966) pp. 180-181 ; amongst later rhetoricians the formula is attested towards the end of the fifteenth century by the curious Italian historian Philippus Callimachus, *Rhetorica* (ed. C. F. Kumaniecki [Warsaw, 1950] p. 24, l. 11).

[8] See H. Bruhn, *Specimen vocabularii rhetorici ad inferioris aetatis Latinitatem pertinens* (diss. Marburg, 1911) ch. 1 ; H. Beumann, *Widukind von Korvei* (Weimar, 1950) pp. 24 f., and id. " Gregor von Tours und der ' sermo rusticus ' " in *Spiegel der Geschichte, Festgabe M. Braubach* (Münster, 1964), pp. 69-98 ; W. Edelstein, *Eruditio und Sapientia : Weltbild und Erziehung in der Karolingerzeit* (Freiburg im Breisgau, 1965) pp. 49 ff. ; J. Schwietering, *Die Demutsformel mittelhochdeutscher Dichter* (*Abh. d. königl. Ges. d. Wiss. Göttingen, phil.-hist. Kl.*, N.F. Bd. XVII, 3, Berlin 1921).

[9] The *ab iudicum persona* approach is clearly related to the *Auftragstopos*, see Quintilian IV, i, 7 and G. Simon in *Archiv für Diplomatik* IV (1958), pp. 59 ff. : the *ab auditorum persona* method is illustrated by the use of prolepsis—the anticipation of objections, see Simon, ibid., pp. 87 ff.

[10] On the antique, rhetorical background of the *spring-topos*, see W. Ross, " Über den sogenannten Natureingang der Trobadors ", *Romanische Forschungen* LXV (1954), pp. 49 ff.

[11] Cf. J. Spörl, " Das Alte und das Neue im Mittelalter ", *Historisches Jahrbuch* L (1930), 297-341 and 498-524 and W. Freund, *Modernus und andere Zeitbegriffe des Mittelalters* (Köln-Graz, 1957).

[12] See G. Penco, " Significato e funzione dei prologhi nell'agiografia Benedettina ", *Aevum* XL (1966), 468-476 ; H. Beumann, " Der Schriftsteller und seine Kritiker im frühen Mittelalter ", *Studium Generale* XII (1959), 503 ; Cf. Edelstein, op. cit., pp. 88 ff.

[13] Beumann, Der Schriftsteller, p. 502. See also Foerster, *Yvain* ed. (1906), p. XIX ; L. W. Kahn, " Rudolf von Ems' Der guote Gerhard. Truth and Fiction in Medieval Epics ", *Germ. Rev.* XIV (1939), esp. 208-210. So developed was the idea of authority and tradition as a cover for implausibility or novelty of matter that fictitious source citations became something of a commonplace, see F. Wilhelm, " Antike und Mittelalter : Studien zur Literaturgeschichte I. Ueber fabulistische Quellenangaben ", *PBB* XXXIII (1908), 286-339.

[14] In a poem of Stephen of Tournai, ed. L. Auvray, *Mélanges Fabre*, we read in one of the quatrains on Rhetoric, ll. 141-2, " Per adjuncta roborat vim probationis, / alia negociis, alia personis."

[15] Cf. Fortunatianus, *Ars. Rhet.*, ed. cit. II, 14, " Exordium genus est, principium et insinuatio species sunt eius." The doctrine of the subtle, indirect approach (*insinuatio*, ἔφοδος) occupies little place in the writings of the Greek rhetoricians and seems scarcely to have been considered by them. It is not unlikely that its survival as a regular part of rhetorical teaching in the late Empire is primarily due to the authority of the *De inventione*. See E. W. Bower, " ΕΦΟΔΟΣ and Insinuatio in Greek and Latin Rhetoric ", *The Classical Quarterly*, NS VIII (1958), 224-230.

[16] See M. L. Clarke, op. cit. ; A. Gwynn, *Roman Education from Cicero to Quintilian* (Oxford, 1926) ; D. L. Clark, *Rhetoric in Greco-Roman Education* (New York, 1957) ; A. D. Leeman, *Orationis Ratio*, 2 vols. (Amsterdam, 1963) ; H. I. Marrou, *Histoire de l'éducation dans l'antiquité* (Paris, 1948) ; see also R. R. Ruether, *Gregory of Nazianzus, Rhetor and Philosopher* (Oxford, 1969), introduction.

[17] The old view is represented by the detailed but very negative study of M. Roger *L'enseignement des lettres classiques d'Ausone à Alcuin* (Paris, 1905) and by G. Kaufmann, " Rhetorenschulen und Klosterschulen oder heidnische und christliche Cultur in Gallien während des 5 und 6 Jahrhunderts ", *Hist. Taschenbuch* (ed. von Raumer), IV (Leipzig, 1869), 1-94. It is rejected by later scholars whose work emphasizes the persistence of the rhetorical tradition, see T. Haarhoff, *Schools of Gaul : A Study of Pagan and Christian Education in the Last Century of the Western Empire* (London, 1920), pp. 157 ff. ; Marrou, op. cit., pp. 398-461 ; P. Riché, *L'éducation et culture dans l'occident barbare VIe - VIIIe siècles* (Paris, 1962) ; H. Pirenne, "De l'état de l'instruction des laïques à l'époque mérovingienne ", *Revue bénédictine* XLVI (1934), 165-177 ; E. Lesne, " La contribution des églises et monastères de l'ancienne Gaule au sauvetage des lettres antiques ", *Rev. d'hist. de l'égl. de France* XXIII (1937), 476-485 ; V. M. O. Denk, *Geschichte des gallo-fränkischen Unterrichts- und Bildungswesens* (Mainz, 1892) ; M. B. Ogle, " Some Aspects of Mediaeval Latin Style ", *Speculum* I (1926), 170-189. On the continuity of the rhetorical tradition in letter writing see H. Liebeschütz in *Archiv für Kulturgeschichte* XXXV (1953), pp. 248 f. On rhetoric in Gaul cf. N. K. Chadwick, *Poetry and Letters in Early Christian Gaul* (London, 1955) and for the use made of Cicero, H. Hagendahl, *Latin Fathers and the Classics* (Göteborg, 1958).

[18] See K. F. Stroheker, *Der senatorische Adel im spätantiken Gallien* (Tübingen, 1948), pp. 130 ff.

[19] See *Loup de Ferrières, Correspondance* ed. L. Levillain (Paris, 1927/1935), t. I, p. 6 ; t. II, pp. 122, 80, and for English translation, G. W. Regenos, *The Letters of Lupus of Ferrières* (The Hague, 1966), pp. 3, 120, 106.

[20] Personal communication to Prof. W. M. Lindsay, dated 26 January 1931. For further details on the work and influence of Lupus see C. H. Beeson, *Lupus of Ferrières as Scribe and Text Critic* (Cambr. Mass., 1930) and Edelstein, op. cit., pp. 169 ff. Beeson's work on Julian of Toledo confirms the importance of France in the 8th and 9th C. for the transmission of Latin texts : see Beeson, "The Ars grammatica of Julian of

Toledo ", *Studi e Testi* XXXVII, *Misc. F. Ehrle*, vol. I (Roma, 1924), 50-70 and cf. Lesne, art. cit. pp. 483 f.

[21] See B. Bischoff, " Hadoard und die Klassikerhandschriften aus Corbie " in id., *Mittelalterliche Studien*, Bd. 1 (Stuttgart, 1966), pp. 49-63.

[22] See L. Wallach, *Alcuin and Charlemagne* : *Studies in Carolingian History and Literature* (Ithaca, N.Y., 1959), pp. 94-95 and cf. id., " Education and Culture in the Tenth Century ", *Medievalia et Humanistica* IX (1955), 18-22. A. Appuhn, *Das Trivium und Quadrivium in Theorie und Praxis*, Teil I (diss. Erlangen, 1900), p. 91 points out that Alcuin would scarcely have been intelligible, without the reader consulting Cicero, copies of whose works could be and evidently were enthusiastically procured in the ninth and tenth centuries.

[23] See J. Egli (ed.) *Der Liber Benedictionum Ekkeharts IV*, (St Gallen, 1909), pp. 205 ff., and see pp. xxvi f. for Ekkehard's knowledge of the rhetoricians and grammarians.

[24] See the references to copies of the Ad Her., Cicero and Quintilian in E. Lesne, *Histoire de la propriété ecclésiastique en France* : t. IV, *Les Livres* : " *scriptoria* " *et bibliothèques du commencement du VIIIe siècle à la fin du XIe* (Lille, 1938) and t. V, *Les écoles de la fin du VIIIe siècle à la fin du XIIe* (Lille, 1940); J. B. Mullinger, *The Schools of Charles the Great* (London, 1877), pp. 83-4 et passim ; R. R. Bolgar, *The Classical Heritage and its Beneficiaries* (Cambridge, 1958) ; M. L. W. Laistner, *Thought and Letters in Western Europe*, A.D. 500-900, (London, 1957) ; J. E. Sandys, *A History of Classical Scholarship* (Cambridge, 1903), vol. I, pp. 623-7 and 630-632 ; J. Fleckenstein, *Die Bildungsreform Karls des Grossen* (Bigge, 1953), pp. 79 f. et passim.

[25] See entries in G. Becker, *Catalogi bibliothecarum antiqui* (Bonn, 1885), and T. Gottlieb, *Ueber Mittelalterliche Bibliotheken* (Leipzig, 1890), and id., *Mittelalterliche Bibliothekskataloge Österreichs*, Bde 1-2 (Wien, 1915-29) ; M. Manitius, " Handschriften antiker Autoren in mittelalterlichen Bibliothekskatalogen ", in *Zentralblatt für Bibliothekswesen*, Beiheft LXVII (1935), pp. 16-18, 19-39, 131-134 ; P. Lehmann, *Beiträge zur mittelalterlichen Bibliotheks-und Überlieferungsgeschichte*, *Bay. Akad. d. Wiss. phil.-hist. Kl.*, *Sitzungsberichte* (1964), Heft IV, esp. p. 7 ; id., *Mittelalterliche Bibliothekskataloge Deutschlands und der Schweiz*, Bde 1-2 (München, 1918-28), Bd. 3 (-4) ed. P. Ruf (München, 1932-62) ; J. W. Thompson, *The Medieval Library* (Chicago, 1939) passim ; A. Viscardi, *Storia Letteraria d'Italia* : *Le Origini*, 3rd. ed. (Milano, 1957) pp. 474 ff. ; L. Delisle, *Le Cabinet des manuscrits de la bibliothèque nationale*, *Histoire générale de Paris*, t, II, (Paris, 1874) pp. 427-550 ; J. S. Beddie, " The Ancient Classics in the Mediaeval Libraries ", *Speculum* V (1930), 3-20. The appellation " (*de*) *Rhetorica Ciceronis* " in these catalogues usually refers to the *De inventione*, occasionally to *Ad Her.*

[26] " . . . primam Tullii rethoricam et librum ad Herrennium et Tullium de oratore et causas Quintiliani et Quintilianum de oratoris institucione." Authorship is attributed by the editor, C. H. Haskins, to Alexander Neckam. See " A List of Text-books from the close of the Twelfth Century ", *Harvard Studies in Classical Philology* XX (1909) p. 92. A revised version of this article appears in Haskins, *Studies in the History of Medieval Science* (Cambr., Mass., 1924) pp. 356-376. The reference to " *causas Quintiliani* " indicates the pseudo-Quintilian declamations, which have been edited by C. Ritter (Leipzig, 1884) and G. Lehnert, (Leipzig, 1905) and which are also attested in medieval library catalogues.

[27] For text see, W. H. D. Suringar, *Historia critica scholiastarum latinorum* (Leiden, 1834), pars prima pp. 213-253, who considered authorship of the text to be uncertain. Excerpts were published by P. Thomas, " Un commentaire du moyen âge sur la rhétorique de Cicéron " in *Mélanges Graux* (Paris, 1884), pp. 41-45. Textual improvements have been suggested by F. Masai, in *Scriptorium V* (1951), 117-120 and 308-309. See also N. M. Haring, " Thierry of Chartres and Dominicus Gundissalinus ", *Med. Stud.* XXVI (1964), 271-286. For a " commentarius in Ciceronis Rhetorica " of the 11th or 12th C. see Ms. Darmst. 2170 at Cologne and, for details, P. Jaffé and G. Wattenbach, *Ecclesie Metropolitanae Coloniensis codices manuscripti* (Berolini, 1874), pp. 83-84. The authority of *De inventione* finds much earlier confirmation in the commentaries on it by Victorinus and Grillius.

[28] See M. T. d'Alverny, *Alain de Lille* : *textes inédits* (Paris, 1965), pp. 52 ff. The identification of the author with Alain de Lille is disputed by some critics.

[29] See Caplan, ed. p. xxv and K. Manitius, " Zur Überlieferung des sogenannten Auctor ad Herennium ", *Philologus* C (1956), 62-66. I regret that I have been unable to consult D. E. E. Grosser, *Studies in the Influence of the Rhetorica Ad Herennium and Cicero's De inventione*, unpubl. diss. (Cornell, 1953).

[30] Letter CI, *Migne PL*, CCVII, col. 313. Wibald, abbot of Corvey, exhorts his friend Manegoldus in a letter of the year 1149, " Lege Quintilianum de institutione oratoria, qui ab utero matris susceptum infantem limare incipit et formare in oratoris perfecti substantiam." Letter CXLVII, *Migne PL* CLXXXIX, col. 1254.

[31] See F. H. Colson, *M. Fabii Quintiliani Institutionis Oratoriae Lib. I* (Cambridge, 1924) introd., pp. xliii-lvi ; P. Lehmann, " Die Institutio Oratoria des Quintilianus im Mittelalter ", *Philologus* LXXXIX (1934), 349-383 ; A. Mollard, " La diffusion de l'Institution oratoire au XIIe siècle ", *Le Moyen Age*, NS V, (1934), 161-175 and ibid. NS VI, (1935), 1-9 ; P. Boskoff, " Quintilian in the Late Middle Ages ", *Speculum* XXVII (1952), 71-78. Professor E. Vinaver in his introduction to *The Works of Sir Thomas Malory* (Oxford, 1947), p. lxiv, has shown how the tradition of Quintilian was preserved in Sidonius Apollinaris, on whose importance for medieval literary technique see, E. Faral, " Sidoine Apollinaire et la technique littéraire du Moyen Age ", in *Msc. G. Mercati*, vol. II (Studi e Testi, 122 [Città del Vaticano, 1946]), pp. 567-580.

[32] Cf. B. Bischoff, " Die Europäische Verbreitung der Werke Isidors von Sevilla ", in id., *Mittelalterliche Studien*, Bd. I (Stuttgart, 1966), pp. 171-194.

[33] For citations of *Ad Her.*, Cicero and Quintilian see A. Gagnér, *Florilegium Gallicum : Untersuchungen und Texte zur Geschichte der mittellateinischen Florilegienliteratur* (Lund, 1936) pp. 121-23, and P. W. Sutherland, *The Use of Quintilian in the Medieval Florilegia*, diss. (North Carolina, 1950) ; B. L. Ullman, " Classical Authors in Certain Mediaeval ' Florilegia ' ", *Class. Phil.* XXVII (1932), 1-42 ; We must often assume lost intermediaries between, for example, the *De inventione* and surviving medieval treatises on rhetoric but the Ciceronian foundation is never in dispute, see P. Abelson, *The Seven Liberal Arts* (New York, 1906), c. 5. and L. M. de Rijk, " On the Curriculum of the Arts of the Trivium at St Gall from c. 850-c. 1000 ", *Vivarium* I (1963), 35-86, esp. 52, 55-56, 65-66, 82.

[34] The rhetorical works under discussion are included in a number of compendia of this type described by E. M. Sandford, " The Use of Classical Latin Authors in the Libri Manuales ", *Transactions and Proceedings of the American Philological Association* LV (1924), 190-248.

[35] For *Artes dictandi* see N. Valois, *De arte scribendi epistolas apud gallicos medii aevi scriptores rhetoresve . . .* diss. (Paris, 1880) ; Rockinger, op. cit. ; C. H. Haskins, *Studies in Mediaeval Culture* (Oxford, 1929), c. ix, pp. 170-192 ; id., " An Early Bolognese Formulary ", *Mélanges H. Pirenne* (Bruxelles, 1926), pp. 201-210 ; A. Bütow, *Die Entwicklung der mittelalterlichen Briefsteller bis zur Mitte des zwölften Jahrhunderts* (diss. Greifswald, 1908) ; F-J. Schmale, *Die Precepta prosaici dictaminis secundum Tullium und die Konstanzer Briefsammlung* (diss. Bonn, 1950) ; Despite its rather dry character *ars dictaminis* was never completely divorced from literary study and contributed in no small measure to the rhetorical formation of many writers, see A. Schiaffini, *Tradizione e poesia nella prosa d'arte Italiana dalla latinità medievale a G. Boccaccio* (Roma, 1943) and J. E. Seigel, *Rhetoric and Philosophy in Renaissance Humanism* (Princeton, 1968), p. 208. For the influence of professional *dictamen* on the poetry of the *rimatori*, see H. Wieruszowski, " Arezzo as a Center of Learning and Letters in the Thirteenth Century ", *Traditio* IX (1953), 376 f. In a study of a *Summa de arte dictandi* ascribed to one Galfridus, F. J. Worstbrock identifies the author with Geoffrey of Vinsauf and concludes (p. 551) " So dürfte sich erneut der Zusammenhang zwischen Ars dictandi und Poetria bestätigen, ein, wie die Summa Bernardi und das Wort Gervasius von Melkley über seinen Vorgänger Bernhard Silvestris bezeugen, für die mittelalterliche Poetik ursprünglicher und fundamentaler Zusammenhang ", *Deutsches Archiv für Erforschung des Mittelalters* XXIII (1967), 549-52 : For texts consult E. Faral, " Le manuscrit 511 du ' Hunterian Museum ' de Glasgow ", *Studi Medievali*, NS IX (1936), 18-121. In its origins, for example with Alberic of Monte Cassino, *dictamen* was simply part of rhetoric, see F-J. Schmale, " Die Bologneser Schule der Ars dictandi ", *Deutsches Archiv für Erforschung des Mittellalters* XIII (1957), 16-34, esp. 26. Probably Alberic himself used a text of *Ad Her.* directly, for one had been copied at Monte Cassino about the time Alberic was writing and is now in Florence (Bibl. Laurent, LI 10), see H. M. Willard in *Haskins Anniversary studies* (New York, 1929), p. 359, note 28. From beginnings in Bologna *ars dictandi* spread rapidly to cities of N. Italy, e.g. Pavia (Henricus Francigena), Cremona, Asti, etc., and thence to France and elsewhere. See G. Vecchi, *Il magistero delle " artes " latine a Bologna nel medioevo* (Bologna, 1958). The early *artes* survive almost exclusively in French and German MSS. In the 1180s we have the school of Orleans—a new centre of *ars dictandi* which drew heavily on the work of Henricus Francigena. Most of the *artes* assume a good knowledge of rhetoric on the part of the reader/pupil. See also J. J. Murphy, " The Arts of Discourse 1050-1400 ", *Med. Stud.* XXIII (1961), 194-205.

[36] On *ars poetica* see E. Faral, *Les arts poétiques du XIIe et du XIIIe siècle* (Paris, repr. 1958) ; H. Brinkmann, *Zu Wesen und Form mittelalterlicher Dichtung* (Halle, 1928), pp. 29-81 ; J. W. H. Atkins, *English Literary Criticism : The Medieval Phase* (Cambridge, 1943) ; C. S. Baldwin, *Medieval Rhetoric and Poetic* (New York, 1928 and repr. Glouc., Mass., 1959) ; M. B. Ogle, art. cit. ; A. C. Spearing, *Criticism and Medieval Poetry* (London, 1964), c. III ; still of great importance, especially for quotations from unpublished MSS., is the study of C. Thurot in *Notices et extraits des manuscrits de la bibl. impériale*, t. 22 (1868) pt. 2, pp. 1-592. See also D. Kelly, " The Scope of the Treatment of Composition in the Twelfth- and Thirteenth-Century Arts of Poetry ", *Speculum* XLI (1966), 270 ff. Kelly argues, rightly I think, that Geoffrey's Poetria was regarded as a Rhetoric.

[37] See Th. Charland, *Artes Praedicandi* (Paris/Ottawa 1936) ; H. Caplan, " Rhetorical Invention in some Mediaeval Tractates on Preaching ", *Speculum* II (1927), 284-95 ; id., " Classical Rhetoric and the Mediaeval Theory of Preaching ", *Classical Philology* XXVIII (1933), 73-96 ; C. Smyth, *The Art of Preaching 747-1939* (London, 1940) ; E. de Bruyne, *Études d'esthétique médiévale*, II (Brugge, 1946), pp. 51 ff. ; Alain de Lille, *Summa de arte praedicatoria*, *Migne PL*, CCX, col. 110-198.

[38] Wrongly attributed by Rockinger and others to Alberic of Monte Cassino, see H. Kalbfuss, " Eine Bologneser Ars dictandi des XII Jahrhunderts ", in *Quellen und Forschungen aus italienischen Archiven und Bibliotheken* XVI (1914), No. 2, p. 6 and C. H. Haskins, *Studies in Medieval Culture*, p. 181. I have not seen L. Secchiari's Bologna University thesis, *Alberico di Montecassino e il problema dell'attribuzione delle " Rationes,"* 1958.

[39] In his account Bütow relies mainly on the Leipzig MS. which he erroneously regarded as representing the work of Henricus Francigena. Cf. E. H. Kantorowicz, " Anonymi ' Aurea Gemma ' ", *Medievalia et Humanistica* I (1943), 41-57.

[40] Cicero's teaching on the *insinuatio* is discussed in a letter written probably at Verdun in the last quarter of the 11th C., see *Die Regensburger rhetorischen Briefe*, *N.31* in *Briefsammlungen der Zeit Heinrichs IV*, bearbeitet von C. Erdmann und N. Fickermann, *MGH, Die Deutschen Geschichtsquellen des M-As, 500-1500* (Weimar, 1950), pp. 364 ff. For the distinction between *principium/insinuatio* drawn from *Ad Her.* see A. Wilmart, " L' 'ars arengandi ' de Jacques de Dinant ", in *Analecta Reginensia*, Studi e testi 59 (Città del Vaticano, 1933), p. 123. However, in the *Ars poetica* of Gervase of Melkley (ed. H-J. Gräbener, Münster, 1965, pp. 226-28) the terms *exordium* and *insinuatio* do not appear to be distinguished. Gräbener's edition, it may be remarked, is full of inaccuracies, see Worstbrock, *Anz. f. d. A.* LXXVIII (1967), 99-107.

[41] For the influence of the *Ad Her.* on the *Rhetorici colores* see L. Wallach, " Onulf of Speyer. A Humanist of the Eleventh Century ", *Medievalia et Humanistica* VI (1950), 35-39.

[42] Sententiae might easily be drawn from compilations like the *Moralium dogma philosophorum*, normally attributed to William of Conches, a French translation of which exists in MSS. of the late 13th C. See J. Holberg, *Das Moralium Dogma Philosophorum des Guillaume de Conches* (Uppsala, 1929). There are frequent citations from *De inventione*. Similar compilations with titles like *sententiae philosophorum* had long existed, see W. Meyer in *Abh. d. Akad. d. Wiss. München, Phil-Philol. Kl.* XVII (1884), pp. 21-22n.

[43] *Scholia Vindobonensia ad Horatii artem Poeticam*, ed. J. Zechmeister (Wien, 1877), p. 5 = scholium on v. 45. On the *ordo artificialis* see Faral, *Les arts poétiques . . .* pp. 55-59. Geoffrey's *Poetria*, an influential work, has been redated, since Faral, to 1200-1202 : see A. Wilmart, " L'art poétique de Geoffroi de Vinsauf et les commentaires de Barthélemy de Pise ", *Revue bénédictine* XLI (1929), 271-275 and *Poetria Nova of Geoffrey of Vinsauf*, tr. M. F. Nims (Toronto, 1967), p. 12. Geoffrey and Matthew are duly named in Hugo von Trimburg's *Registrum multorum auctorum* (c. 1280), a manual of latin authors commonly read in schools.

[44] The terminology used to indicate the *captatio benevolentiae* or introduction might also include *arenga* ("quedam prefacio que ad benivolenciam captandam premittitur" Baumgartenberg Formulary, Rock. II, 744. Cf. Conrad of Mure, Rock I. 467). On this term see M. Granzin, *Die Arenga der frühmittelalterlichen Urkunde* (diss. Halle, 1930), pp. 24-25 ; H. Fichtenau, *Arenga : Spätantike und Mittelalter im Spiegel von Urkundenformeln* (Graz-Köln, 1957), p. 20. Cf. G. Vecchi, " Le Arenge di Guido Faba e l'eloquenza d'arte, civile e politica duecentesca ", *Quadrivium* IV (1960), 61-87.

[45] In the surviving fragments of his *De Comœdia*, VII, 3, ed. P. Weissner, *Aeli Donati, commentum Terenti* (Lipsiae, 1902), vol. 1, p. 27, Donatus' distinction of two types of prologue occupies an intermediate position in the tradition concerning the dual function of prologues. " Inter prologum et prologium quidam hoc interesse voluerunt,

quod prologus est, ubi aut poeta excusatur aut fabula commendatur, prologium autem est, cum tantum de argumento dicitur."

[46] See P. Zumthor, in review of Curtius, Z. f. Rom. Phil. LXVI (1950), 162 ; W. B. Sedgwick, " The Style and Vocabulary of the Latin Arts of Poetry of the Twelfth and Thirteenth Centuries ", Speculum III (1928), 351 ; M. Pelan and I. D. O. Arnold, La partie arthurienne du roman de Brut (Paris, 1962), p. 32 ; R. O. Payne in Companion to Chaucer Studies, ed. B. Rowland (London, 1968), pp. 38-57.

[47] See G. Biller, Étude sur le style des premiers romans français en vers (Göteborg, 1916); R. Grosse, Der Stil von Chrestiens von Troies, Franz. Studien I (1881), 127-260; V. Bertolucci, " Commento retorico all' ' Erec ' e al ' Cliges ' ", Studi mediolatini e volgari VIII (1960), 9-51 ; id., " La retorica nel Tristano di Thomas ", ibid. VI-VII (1959), 25-61 ; R. Baehr, " Studien zur Rhetorik in den Rime Guittones von Arezzo ", Z. f. Rom. Phil. LXXIII (1957), 193-258 and 357-413, ibid., LXXIV (1958), 163-211 ; G. Ehrismann, Studien über Rudolf von Ems (Heidelberg, 1919) ; S. Sawicki, Gottfried von Strassburg und die Poetik des Mittelalters (Berlin, 1932) ; P. B. Salmon, The works of Hartmann von Aue in the light of Medieval Poetics, unpubl. diss. (London, 1957).

[48] See Sawicki, op. cit., pp. 54-55 and G. Chiri, L'Epica latina medioevale e la Chanson de Roland (Genova, 1936), pp. 56 f.

[49] See Sawicki, op. cit., pp. 23 ff. and R. Gruenter, " Über den Einfluss des Genus iudicale auf den höfischen Redestil ", DVJS XXVI (1952), 49-57 (Hartmann's rhetorical instruction contained traditional elements of forensic oratory).

[50] See E. R. Curtius, " Mittelalter-Studien XVIII ", Z. f. Rom. Phil. LXIII (1943), 245-256 ; R. Halpersohn, Über die Einleitungen im altfranzösischen Kunstepos, Heidelberg diss. (Berlin, 1911) ; M. Gsteiger, " Note sur les préambules des chansons de geste ", CCM II (1959), 213-20 ; H. Schreiber, Studien zum Prolog in mittlalterlicher Dichtung, Bonn diss. (Würzburg, 1935) ; R. Ritter, Die Einleitungen der altdeutschen Epen (diss. Bonn, 1908) ; G. Simon, " Untersuchungen zur Topik der Widmungsbriefe . . .", Archiv für Diplomatik IV (1958), 52-119 and ibid., V-VI (1959-60), 73-153 ; B. Boesch Die Kunstanschauung in der mhd. Dichtung (Bern and Leipzig, 1936) ; R. Dragonetti, La technique poétique des trouvères dans la chanson courtoise (Brugge, 1960) ; P. J. Jones, Prologue and Epilogue in Old French Lives of Saints before 1400, diss. Pennsylvania (Philadelphia, 1933).

[51] On education in Troyes, 1152-1181, see H. D'Arbois de Jubainville, Histoire des ducs et des comtes de Champagne, t. III (Paris, 1861), pp. 184 ff. Wolfram von Eschenbach (Parzival, 827, 1) refers to Chrétien as " von Troys meister Cristjân." On education generally in the 12th C see G. Paré, A. Brunet, P. Tremblay, La renaissance du XIIe siècle : les écoles et l'enseignement (Paris/Ottawa, 1933) ; P. Riché, " Recherches sur l'instruction des laïcs du IXe au XIIe siècle ", CCM V (1962), 175-182 ; A. Vàrvaro, " Scuola e cultura in Francia nel XII secolo ", Studi mediolatini e volgari X (1962), 299-330; P. Delhaye, " L'organisation scolaire au XIIe siècle ", Traditio V (1947), 211-68 ; P. Abelson, op. cit. ; F. A. Specht, Geschichte des Unterrichtswesens in Deutschland . . . (Stuttgart, 1885).

[52] I cite from the edition of T. B. W. Reid (Manchester, repr. 1952), though making use of Foerster's 1887 ed. For the sake of brevity I refer to the work as Yvain.

[53] M. Klose, Der Roman von Claris und Laris . . . Z. f. Rom. Phil. Beiheft LXIII (1916), p. 167.

[54] J. Frappier, Le roman breton : Yvain ou le chevalier au lion, C.D.U. (Paris, 1952), p. 6.

[55] W. Kellermann, Aufbaustil und Weltbild Chrestiens von Troyes im Percevalroman, Z. f. Rom. Phil. Beiheft LXXXVIII (1936), p. 36.

[56] Small ed. 1906, p. xix ". . . so ist der Yvain das einzige Werk Kristians, worin keine Quelle welcher Art immer angegeben wird, wie denn demselben jede Einleitung überhaupt abgeht, etwas so auffälliges, dass man gern eine Verstümmlung des Anfangs annehmen möchte, wenn nicht die Ablenkung auf den orden der echten Amorritter (z. 16-18), dessen treues Mitglied, wie aus der Erzählung erhellt, Ivain ist und der Übergang z. 33 . . . die Stelle auf der in der damaligen Zeit unvermeidlichen Einleitung vertreten würden."

[57] Cf. Gsteiger, art. cit., p. 216, " Impressionner à l'avance l'auditoire, l'influencer dans un sens positif, on reconnaît là une variante—un peu grossière, il est vrai—de la captatio benevolentiae prescrite par la rhétorique antique."

[58] The comparability of the position of the orator before his audience with the oral recitation of a romance by a poet to his public need hardly be underlined.

[59] Art. cit., p. 213.

[60] See ed. W. M. Lindsay, repr. 1961, p. 115, " What appears to us garrulous prolixity in some of the prologues of Plautus was due to the practical necessity of securing the attention and the intelligence of a restless crowd of holiday-seekers."

[61] Considerations of space compel me to refer the reader to the exposition in the earlier part of this paper for a proper understanding of what follows.

[62] The epithet " buen " applied to Arthur stems from Geoffrey of Monmouth's reference to his *bonitas*, *Historia Regum*, IX, i, and Wace, *Brut* (ed. Arnold), l. 8735. It soon became a stock appellation, see Hermann zur Jacobsmühlen, *Zur Charakteristik des könig Artus im altfrz. Kunstepos* (diss. Marburg, 1888), p. 45. The *vir bonus* for Cicero was a man embodying all the virtues (see *Tusc.* V, x, 28) but the origins of this use of the epithet may have been religious (see introductory lines of the *Eulalie* and *Voyage de St Brendan*) and here the presentation of Arthur for *imitatio* is more reminiscent of the hagiographer than of the historian. Arthur's *proesce* probably derives from Wace (*Brut.*, 11. 8736 [Ms.J], 9786).

[63] The setting is part of a tradition which goes back to Geoffrey's description of the coronation of Arthur and the latter's generosity soon becomes a regular feature (*Brut.*, ll. 10485-10495). " Li riches rois " is a common epithet applied to Arthur in the romances, see Jacobsmühlen, loc. cit.

[64] See *Neophilologus* XLIII (1959), 288-291. Locke appears to have been unaware of the fact that the suggestion had already been made by E. Philipot in *Annales de Bretagne* VIII (1892-93), p. 477.

[65] For a reference to the Greek etymology see Philippe de Thaun's remarks on " pantere " in his bestiary ed. Walberg, ll. 461 ff. (l. 465, " Pan en griu trestut est "). For etymologizing by hagiographers see Jones, op. cit., c. III, and by the *dictatores* of 13th C. Italy, Wieruszowski, art. cit., p. 362.

[66] For Quintilian's conception of *urbanitas* as wit spiced with culture and learning see M. A. Grant, *The Ancient Rhetorical Theories of the Laughable* (Madison, 1924), p. 123. On learning and the *cognoscenti* at the court of Champagne see J. W. Thompson, *The Literacy of the Laity in the Middle Ages* (Berkeley, 1939), p. 142 ff. As Foerster remarked (1887 ed. note) the rime *Pantecoste-coste* became proverbial, but note that it had already been used several times in the *Voyage de St Brendan*, ed. Waters, ll. 587-8, 865-6, 1317-18. The text of the *Lai du cor* (c. 1150-70 ?) as contained in Oxford Bodl. Lib., MS. Digby 86, has the same rime (ll. 7-8) but I am inclined to agree with H. Dörner (*Robert Biquet's lai du cor*, diss. [Strassburg, 1907]), who observes that the opening lines have undergone some changes and therefore omits the lines in question from his critical text.

[67] Both *Fergus* (ed. Martin, l. 715) and the *Prose Merlin* have " Carduel en Gales " indicating, as in Chretien, Carlisle. Carduel, as Arthur's seat, seems to stem from Marie de France, see M. Delbouille, " Caerlïon et Cardueil, sièges de la cour d'Arthur ", *Neophil. Mitt.* LXVI (1965), 436-446. Cf. P. Rickard, *Britain in Medieval French Literature 1100-1500* (Cambridge, 1956), pp. 101-102 n[6].

[68] See J. A. W. Bennett, *The Parlement of Foules* (Oxford, 1957), pp. 26-27, and cf. *Sir Gawain and the Green Knight*, l. 1507. *Amors* (l. 13) I take to be singular, with J. Frappier, *Romania* LXXXVIII (1967), p. 461.

[69] See prologues of *Blancandrin* (ed. Michelant), *Claris et Laris* (ed. Alton), *Florimont* (ed. Hilka, ll. 53-60) and *Dolopathos* (ed. Brunet and Montaiglon).

[70] Gsteiger, art. cit., p. 219, n. 54, declares, rightly in my opinion, " Il est possible que la rhétorique antique ait influencé ces polémiques."

[71] Marie's authorship has recently been disputed by R. Baum, *Recherches sur les œuvres attribuées à Marie de France* (Heidelberg, 1968), p. 135.

[72] The introductory section is constructed primarily of the figures of *traductio* (proesce/preu ; coste/pantecoste ; amors/amer ; mantent/mançonge) and *contentio* (ll. 12-13, 14-15, 17-18, 21/24, 16, 29-30, 32). The antithetical structure contributes the perspective of the prologue. Antithesis had, of course, received a tribute from St Augustine as the most decent and effective of rhetorical figures, see *De Civitate Dei*, ed. B. Dombart (Lipsiae, 1905-1909), vol. I, bk, XI, c. 18.

[73] See *Renaud de Montauban* (ed. Michelant), p. 181, l. 16, " Miex vaut morir à honor que vivre a deshonor " ; *Buevon de Conmarchis* (ed. Henry), l. 499, " Mieus vaut mors à honneur que ne fait honteus vis " ; *Les Enfances Ogier* (ed. Henry), ll. 2923-4, " Mieus vaut hom mors et preudon apelés/Que ne fait vis qui est deshonnourés ". Cf. E. Ebert, *Die Sprichwörter der altfrz. Karlsepen* (diss. Marburg, 1884). Professor Reid (*Yvain* ed., p. 187) points out the similarity of the sententia in *Yvain*, ll. 31-32, to one contained in Morawski's collection : see J. Morawski, *Proverbes français antérieurs au*

XVe siècle (Paris, 1925), nr. 1257, " Mieux vault co(u)rtois mort que vilain vif ". Cf. nr. 1271, " Mius vaut morir a joe que vivre a onte ".

[74] See Wace, *Brut.*, ll. 13, 279 f. The same belief is expressed by the author of *Durmart le Galois*, ed. Gildea, ll. 15939-40, " li bons rois Artus est fenis, / mais encore dure ses pris " and by the troubador Cerveri, see *Mélanges Delbouille* II, p. 96. The author of the Provençal *Jaufré* talks of Arthur's fame in similar terms to Chrétien, " Tant fu pros e de gran valor / que ja no morra sa lausor, / car jasempre serant retraxas / las prosezas qe el a faxas / eil bos cavaliers mentagutz / qe a sa cort foron elegutz . . ." (ed. Brunel, ll. 27-32). G. Ehrismann, *Gesch. der dtsch. Lit.* II, 2, 1, p. 134, ascribes to Guibert de Nogent a report of this belief of the Bretons.

[75] Donatus in *De Comoedia* VII, 2 ed. cit. describes four types of *prologus* : " commendativus, quo poeta vel fabula commendatur ; relativus, quo aut adversario maledictum aut populo gratiae referentur ; argumentativus, exponens fabulae argumentum ; mixtus, omnia haec in se continens." In the light of these definitions the *prologus* to *Yvain* would have to be described as *mixtus*, for it contains the commendation of Arthur and his Knights, the denigration of false lovers, and some suggestion of the theme of love (this is really an artifice to secure the audience's goodwill for the romance is not fundamentally about love).

[76] The main *topos* is of Biblical origin, see Matthew 13, 15 ff. *Jaufré* (ed. Brunel, ll. 17 ff.) contains a very similar speech.

[77] The conscientious but abbreviating copyist of the Vatican manuscript of the *Yvain* evidently viewed the speech as a unit and decided to cut it.

[78] Cf. C. Foulon, " Le Rou de Wace, l'Yvain de Chrétien de Troyes et Eon de l'Étoile ", *BBSIA* XVII (1965), 93.

[79] This is characteristic of Chrétien's method in several of his romances. I hope to return to this in a further article on Chrétien's prologues and those of his translators.

[80] Op. cit., p. 71. Cf. H. Hunger, *Prooimion : Elemente der Byzantinischen Kaiseridee in den Arengen der Urkunden* (Wien, 1964), esp. pp. 211 ff. (" Propaganda im Prooimion ").

[81] J. M. Steadman, " ' Courtly Love ' as a Problem of Style ", in *Chaucer und seine Zeit* ; *Symposion für Walther F. Schirmer* (Tübingen, 1968), pp. 1-33. See also F. Quadlbauer, *Die antike Theorie der genera dicendi im lateinischen Mittelalter* (Sitzungsb., Österreich. Akad. d. Wiss., phil.-hist. Kl., 241 [Wien, 1962]).

[82] It is curious that whilst there is no evidence that Latin rhetoricians regarded the *insinuatio* as anything other than an alternative to the *prooemium*, some Greek rhetoricians seem to have thought of the ἔφοδος as additional to or existing alongside the *prooemium*. See Bower art. cit., 227 f.

[83] In this article I have used the following abbreviations :
Halm, C. Halm, *Rhetores latini minores*, 2 fascicules (Lipsiae, 1863).
Rockinger, L. Rockinger, *Briefsteller und Formelbücher des eilften bis vierzehnten Jahrhunderts* (Quellen und Erörterungen zur bayerischen und deutschen Geschichte, Bd. IX, München, 1863).
I cite from the following editions :
Ad. C. Herennium Libri IV de ratione dicendi, ed. & tr. H. Caplan (Loeb Classical Library. London, 1954).
De inventione . . . ed. & tr. H. M. Hubbell (Loeb Classical Library. London, 1949).
Quintilian, Institutio Oratoria, ed. & tr. H. E. Butler (Loeb Classical Library, 4 vols. London, 1953).

II

SOME THOUGHTS ON THE *SENS* OF
LE CHEVALIER DE LA CHARRETTE[1]

Since Gaston Paris's article on Lancelot appeared in *Romania* in 1883, it has been customary for literary historians to interpret Chrétien de Troyes's *Chevalier de la Charrette* as written in praise of the Provençal ideal of *fin'amors*. Though they express reservations, Cross and Nitze, Frappier and, still more recently, F. Douglas Kelly, in his very detailed and valuable study of the romance, have come to conclusions very similar to those of Gaston Paris, and there are few who have questioned this interpretation in any detail.[2] When I had occasion to read *Le Chevalier de la Charrette* recently, however, I came to have doubts about the main emphasis of this view. I am not denying, of course, that Lancelot and Guenevere's relationship is governed by the conventions of *fin'amors*, for does not Chrétien actually apply the term *fin amant* to Lancelot, the only time that he uses it in his romances ?[3] What I believe to be less certain is the view that Guenevere and Lancelot are intended to exemplify a *dompna* and her lover according to the Provençal ideal. If my reading of the romance is correct, it contains criticism, implicit as well as explicit, of both characters' behaviour. With this in mind I am going to study Lancelot and Guenevere, at least in their attitudes and actions towards each other, and to examine some of Chrétien's own comments about them. I shall then consider whether they tally with the widely accepted view that *Le Chevalier de la Charrette* glorifies the Provençal ideal of adulterous love in which the lover is subjected to his mistress's every whim. I agree with Douglas Kelly that Godefroi de Leigni's closing lines must be taken at their face value and that he completed the romance according to Chrétien's wishes, observing scrupulously the latter's intentions.[4] I therefore propose to take the whole romance as a unit and to treat evidence in the last thousand lines to be as reliable as that provided by the first six thousand. Critics have tended to neglect Godefroi de Leigni's contribution

[1] This article was delivered as a paper at the Ninth International Arthurian Congress held at Cardiff in August 1969. All references to the texts of *Le Chevalier de la Charrette* and *Cligés* are to the Classiques Français du Moyen Âge editions by Mario Roques and A. Micha.

[2] T. P. Cross and W. A. Nitze, *Lancelot and Guenevere : A Study on the Origins of Courtly Love*, Chicago, 1930 ; J. Frappier, *Chrétien de Troyes : l'homme et l'œuvre*, Paris, Hatier-Boivin, 1957, 2nd edition, 1968 ; F. Douglas Kelly, *Sens et Conjointure in the " Chevalier de la Charrette "*, The Hague, 1966. Among those to have cast doubts on this interpretation is J. Mandel in his article entitled " Elements in the ' Charrette ' World : The Father-Son Relationship ", *Modern Philology*, LXII (1964-65), 97-104. In a foot-note to his article " The Court of Champagne as a literary center ", *Speculum*, XXXVI (1961), 551-91, J. F. Benton states that he too has questioned it in his Ph.D. thesis which, to my knowledge has remained unpublished, and to which I have not had access.

[3] 3962.

[4] 7098-112.

(i.e. from Lancelot's imprisonment in the tower onwards), considering it unimportant. In my opinion, this part contains much that is essential to the understanding of the *sens*. I shall start with Lancelot, since he dominates the first half of the romance.

Soon after Meleagant and Kay, accompanied by Guenevere, have left Arthur's court for a nearby forest where they are to wage their single combat for the queen, they are followed by Arthur and Gawain, the latter fully armed and provided with two spare chargers. On perceiving Kay's riderless and blood-spattered horse, Gawain rides on alone and is soon met by a knight whose steed is literally on its last legs. This is none other than Lancelot, though his identity will only be revealed later. With the most perfunctory of greetings, he asks Gawain for one of his spare chargers. The choice of either is offered him, but Lancelot leaps on to the nearer one without a glance at the other, and he rides off post-haste without expressing a word of thanks.[5] As Dr Barbara Sargent has pointed out,[6] Lancelot's hurry and lack of courtesy stamp him as a man obsessed. His obsession is confirmed when Gawain, who has come across the charger abandoned dead in the midst of signs of combat, catches up with Lancelot, fully armed but for his lance and following on foot a cart driven by a dwarf.[7] Since this episode gives the romance its title, there is no doubt about its importance to the understanding of the *sens*. Chrétien starts by insisting on the shameful associations of the cart in Arthur's day, when it served as a pillory for the worst criminals. On being told by the driver that if he wishes to receive information about the queen's whereabouts he must climb into the cart, Lancelot, after a moment's hesitation, does so, but his hesitation will later cause a crisis in his relations with the queen. On the other hand, the news of his ride in the cart will precede him, and the reason for it will be misinterpreted by all he meets, bringing on him their mockery, reproaches and abuse. Let us look for a moment at what Chrétien has to say about this action so full of consequences. He tells us that when Lancelot hesitated to do something that would shame him, he was ruled by *raison*. But *amor* quickly overcame *raison*, and since *amor* willed it, Lancelot jumped into the cart. No word of either praise or blame of the action is included, and so Chrétien's account has every appearance of being objective. How does Gawain react to the situation, however ? He asks the dwarf the same question as Lancelot and, on receiving the same reply, he categorically expresses his refusal to jump on to the cart, considering such a course to be *molt grant folie* and the exchange of a knight's charger for a cart with its shameful associations to be *trop vilain*. Chrétien wishes to imply, therefore, that Lancelot has foregone *raison* and committed *folie* at the dictates of *amor*, thus neglecting an important element of *fin'amors*, essential to the chivalrous

[5] 269-95.
[6] Barbara N. Sargent, " L'autre chez Chrétien de Troyes ", *Cahiers de Civilisation médiévale*, X (1967), 199-205.
[7] 304-94.

knight, though sometimes neglected by the *troubadours* themselves in their poems, namely *mesure*.[8] And so Chrétien cannot be using the word *amor* in this context in the sense of *fin'amors*, but in that of " amour passion ", a known source of *folie*, as he does in *Cligés* when referring to Tristan and Isolt.[9] If this is the case, this episode implies criticism of Lancelot's behaviour as a courtly lover for having allowed his feelings for Guenevere to override his reason.

Let us now pass on to the incident which takes place next morning when Lancelot, Gawain and their hostess, who are standing at an upstairs window, watch a funeral procession led by a tall knight accompanied by a lady.[10] Recognizing her as the abducted Guenevere, Lancelot follows her intently with his eyes until she has disappeared. What is significant is Lancelot's paralysis at the sight of the queen instead of an irresistible urge to action in defence of a lady in distress expected of a chivalrous knight. Yet away from Guenevere only a few hours earlier, he had successfully undergone the tests of the forbidden bed and the flaming lance which had provided ample proof of his courage and prowess.[11] Far from inspiring Lancelot to greater deeds of valour, Guenevere's physical presence has strengthened his obsession for her and incapacitated him for knightly duties. The same thing happens when Lancelot is jousting with Meleagant.[12] Weakened by loss of blood resulting from wounds suffered in crossing the sword-bridge the day before, he faces defeat, from which he is saved by a damsel who shouts to him that Guenevere is present. This sudden discovery has such an unsettling effect on him that he gazes intently at the queen while committing the elementary mistake of turning his back on his opponent. It is only when another shout from the damsel brings him back to his senses that he is able to put his chivalry and love for Guenevere into perspective and to complete the near-defeat of Meleagant. But let us return to the funeral procession. Not only is Lancelot incapable of action, but, as the queen disappears from sight, his despairing response is to throw himself out of the window. He is held back by a horrified Gawain, who once more describes his companion's conduct as *folie*. In this incident, therefore, Lancelot again fails to behave with the moderation and restraint expected of a courtly knight and is prevented with difficulty from committing the gravest of sins.

A little further, Gawain and Lancelot separate, each taking a different route to the kingdom of Gorre to which Guenevere has been abducted. Gawain, who has been given the choice of way, decides on the easier one, leaving Lancelot gladly to follow the more difficult but also the shorter road.[13] Lancelot is so engrossed in dreams of his lady-love as he rides on

---

[8] See R. Nelli, *L'Érotique des Troubadours*, Toulouse, 1963, p. 190 ; M. Lazar, *Amour courtois et fin'amors dans la littérature du XIIe siècle*, Paris, 1964, pp. 28-32, 114.

[9] See *Cligés* 3107-9, 3117.

[10] 535-82.

[11] 467-534.

[12] 3584-757.

[13] 644-99.

that he is oblivious of the world around him. He hears, sees, and under-
stands nothing : he has even forgotten his own name, his very existence.[14]
This is the love trance common to the Provençal lyric poet rapt in thoughts
of his *dompna*. In this state, induced by his obsession with Guenevere,
Lancelot arrives at a ford, unaware of the three challenges called out by
the knight who acts as its guardian. Interpreting Lancelot's rêverie as
insolence, the latter attacks, and Lancelot is awakened from his dreams only
when unhorsed in mid-stream. Acutely conscious of the humiliation he has
suffered at the knight's hand, though in reality this is slight compared to
the shame of the cart-ride, Lancelot engages in a fierce combat with him,
emerging victorious, yet angered by the length of time taken for success.[15]
So here the love trance caused by his obsession with Guenevere has brought
Lancelot to the brink of disaster and hindered his progress in his quest for
the queen. Far from continually inspiring her lover as a *dompna* should,
Guenevere is proving on occasion to be a source of weakness, and the fault
lies partly in Lancelot's inability to keep his thoughts of her under control
and within the bounds of the real world around him.

In the next adventure, however, his devotion to the queen does help.
Lancelot has reluctantly accepted a damsel's invitation to spend the night
at her castle on condition that he shares her bed. Inspired by thoughts of
the queen, but this time preventing them from impeding his powers of
action, he goes to rescue the damsel from rape against apparently over-
whelming odds, determined to die with honour rather than live in shame.
His sense of duty as a knight is now strengthened by his love for Guenevere,
and his rapid success is assured. When he lies on the bed with the damsel,
no intercourse takes place, for his thoughts are with the queen, to whom
he remains faithful.[16] I can see no criticism of Lancelot's behaviour here,
only praise for his fidelity, chastity and single-mindedness.

This self-control does not last, however, for when next morning he
departs in the company of his hostess, so obsessed does he become with his
thoughts of Guenevere that he pays scant attention to his companion, thus
breaking one of the basic rules of courtesy towards a lady. By the side of
a fountain lies a comb of gilded ivory in which half a handful of golden hair
has been caught. On picking it up, Lancelot cannot take his eyes off the
hair and feels faint when told it belongs to Guenevere. He carefully extracts
the hair so as not to damage a single strand and starts to venerate it like
the relic of a saint, touching his eyes, lips and forehead with it before placing
it next to his skin above the heart, considering that it will prevent him
from all illnesses more efficaciously than the relics of St Martin or St James.[17]
The veneration of something belonging to a *dompna* as if it had a religious
significance is a well-known characteristic of Provençal love poetry, but

[14] 710-24.
[15] 730-930.
[16] 931-1280.
[17] 1281-494.

what concerns us is Chrétien's attitude towards it in the *Charrette*. No direct criticism is expressed, it is true, but the very extravagance of the hyperbole and comparisons suggest that, as in the cart incident and the attempted suicide, Lancelot's behaviour is lacking in the *mesure* and *raison* expected of a knight in an ideal courtly relationship.

Criticism would also seem to be implied by his conduct at the beginning of the next adventure, in the course of which they meet a knight who has long wished to abduct the damsel. She informs Lancelot that she expects him to protect her against this newcomer, but his mind is so focused on Guenevere that he rudely brushes off the damsel's request as unimportant, neglecting thus one of his knightly duties, always to be prepared to protect a lady. It is only after the damsel has been the victim of the knight's arrogance by his seizure of her bridle and Lancelot himself has been the butt of the knight's scorn that he comes forward in her defence.[18] Would any knight-errant in his right mind allow this to happen ? Once more, Lancelot's obsession for Guenevere has hindered the performance of his chivalrous duties to a lady, to whose aid he had unhesitatingly come the night before.

Such are those of Lancelot's adventures in which his feelings for Guenevere actively intervene in the first part of the romance, and in all of them, with one exception, concentrating his attention on Guenevere proves an impediment to him. He comes closest to the ideal of chivalry when least absorbed in thoughts of his *dompna*, i.e. when he has to concentrate on the situation in hand, such as the protection of the amorous hostess. It is not after thinking of Guenevere but after praying in the chapel that he raises the tombstone, an adventure that shows Lancelot to be already a knight of incomparable prowess ;[19] it is God, not the queen, whom he invokes before attempting to cross the sword-bridge, the supreme test of his physical and moral courage, in which he overcomes the terrors of the mind as well as the suffering of the body, though love helps him to bear the latter.[20] If my interpretation is correct, Chrétien is showing that Lancelot's absorption in Guenevere is excessive, particularly when he is reminded of her physical presence, and that it is detrimental to his prowess. From all the adventures that I have dealt with, I conclude that Chrétien is trying to depict Lancelot as a knight possessing, in addition to the innate qualities required to make him perfect, one serious weakness : he is lacking in a quality considered by Chrétien to be essential to courtly love in a chivalrous setting, namely *mesure*.

This is the point at which I wish to begin considering Guenevere, since it is after Lancelot's crossing of the sword-bridge that she starts to play an active part in the romance. The only previous occasion on which she has done so is the opening scene at Arthur's court, and on that, because the king inexcusably subjected her to humiliation in front of the whole

[18] 1496-633.
[19] 1829-919.
[20] 3084-90.

court, she was cast in the rôle of a *mal-mariée*, entitled by literary convention to find love outside marriage. But how does she measure up to the ideal
of the courtly *dompna*, a model of beauty and virtue, who has to find the
right compromise between *mesure* and *merci*, between granting her favours
too readily and withholding them too long, thereby discouraging her lover ?

I have already discussed Lancelot's behaviour during the first combat
between him and Meleagant after the crossing of the sword-bridge, a combat
attended by the queen.[21] How does she act ? One is immediately struck by
her passivity. It is not she who intervenes to save her lover from certain
defeat, though she alone knows who he is. It is a maiden, unconnected with
Guenevere as far as we can tell, who finds out from her Lancelot's identity
and then draws his attention to the queen's presence. Again it is the maiden
and not Guenevere who brings the hypnotized Lancelot back to his senses
and gives him the practical advice which will allow him to turn the tables
on Meleagant. Guenevere's only intervention, at Bademagu's request, will
stop the combat and prevent Meleagant's defeat, thus impeding Lancelot
in the attainment of his final objective, though he succeeds in winning the
freedom of all the prisoners from Logres, including the queen.[22]

Lancelot now visits the queen in her chamber but, to his amazement,
her face takes on an angry expression and, instead of giving him the sweet
look he deserves for the mortal dangers he has undergone in her service,
she curtly tells him that he can expect no gratitude. Bademagu, who is
the exemplar of courtesy, is incensed by this conduct, which he considers
inexcusable on the part of a lady towards a knight who has served her so
well, and he concludes that it can be explained only if Lancelot has done
her some wrong, which the reader knows to be untrue. As elsewhere in the
second part of the romance, Bademagu's views reflect Chrétien's, I should
say, and I wonder if Guenevere is not being unfavourably contrasted to
him. His generosity and patience towards his unworthy son and vassal
Meleagant are startlingly different from the queen's unwarranted harshness
towards her devoted knight. Astounded and bitterly disappointed though
he is, Lancelot reacts true to type. Showing no anger, he replies most
courteously and submissively in the manner of the *fin amant*, who would
not presume to question the justice meted out by his *dompna*.[23]

A little later Lancelot is taken prisoner while searching for Gawain, but
a rumour reaches the queen that he has been killed. Once alone, full of
remorse, she gives vent to her true feelings and thinks of killing herself. In
reality, she has never had any doubts about Lancelot's undying love for
her, we are told, and so her coldness towards him had been a sin. In a
monologue, she enumerates the offences that she has committed during her
recent meeting with him. By refusing to welcome him with a look or a word,

---

[21] 3584-912.

[22] Guenevere will similarly accede to Bademagu's plea to stop the judicial combat
between Lancelot and Meleagant, once again imperilling Lancelot's life (5010 ff.).

[23] 3924-4001.

not only has she behaved like *une folle*, she states, but she has acted with criminal cruelty. In fact, during the whole of their meeting she was playing a game. She goes on to express her sorrow that they had not experienced intercourse at least once, and ends with a piece of casuistry to convince herself that she will do better to live and suffer than to find peace by taking her life.[24]

Guenevere's remorse is responsible for the extravagant tone of the monologue, but she also expresses genuine awareness of her shortcomings as a *dompna*. According to the conventions of *fin'amors*, Lancelot should have been rewarded for his services, since a *dompna*'s duty was to encourage her lover by gradually bestowing her favours on him.[25] This is probably why, in the middle of the monologue, she expresses regret at not having had intercourse with him, a remark, however, that may also contain an undertone of passion alien to the *mesure* advocated in *fin'amors*, though not always observed by Provençal poets. It is clear from this monologue that Guenevere's true motive for continuing to test Lancelot's love had been to satisfy her pleasure at asserting her dominance over him. This is confirmed a little later when she hears that Lancelot is alive and that he has tried to kill himself because he thought her dead. She is delighted, states Chrétien.[26] Throughout, therefore, she has been more concerned with exercising her authority over her lover than with her true duty to encourage him to attain a higher degree of chivalrous perfection. Guenevere is the first example of the *belle dame sans merci*, and this is a conception of the *dompna* with which Chrétien is clearly out of sympathy.

A comparison between Guenevere's reactions and the way in which Lancelot responds to the rumour that reaches him of the queen's death is significant. Lancelot does not merely talk about committing suicide, as the queen has done; he actually tries to strangle himself and would have been successful but for his companions' intervention.[27] Chrétien certainly wants to show that Lancelot's suffering is far more intense than Guenevere's, lacking though his conduct is in *mesure*, and this is confirmed in the long monologue in which he expresses his despair and tries to explain the queen's displeasure at their last meeting.[28] Concluding that his ride in the cart must be its cause, he expresses surprise that this action should have been misinterpreted by one versed in the art of love. For sure, this is a further implied criticism of the queen, which suggests that she has still something to learn about the way to treat a lover.

On Lancelot's return to Bademagu's court, he is able to ask the queen why she was annoyed with him.[29] She explains that his slight hesitation before climbing into the cart, caused by his shame and fear, had displeased

24 4157-4244.
25 See R. Nelli, op. cit., p. 194.
26 4433.
27 4250-316.
28 4318-96.
29 4455-500.

her, not his ride in the cart. For a second or so he had shown unwillingness, and this she had considered unforgivable. What had really annoyed Guenevere, therefore, was her discovery that Lancelot's subjection to her domination was still incomplete at the time of the cart episode, since he had hesitated before committing a shameful act for her sake. As in their previous encounter Lancelot reacts with total submissiveness : he admits his offence and begs for forgiveness. This is granted by Guenevere, presumably still under the influence of her remorse at not having been more aware of her duties as a *dompna*.

There is nothing to indicate in the romance that Lancelot has ever received from Guenevere a token of her love. All that he possesses of hers is the hair that he has taken from her comb. One would expect the queen, under the influence of *fin'amors*, to give Lancelot a ring or some other token at this point as an indication that she had accepted him as her lover. But she does no such thing. On the other hand, she grants him a secret assignation for the following night. Very discreetly Guenevere tells Lancelot to come outside her window when everyone is in bed, though insisting that he must not enter since Kay will be asleep inside. True to the courtly convention, she begs Lancelot to make sure he is not watched.[30] What is surprising, however, is the sudden haste with which this next step of the courtship is reached, and it seems to reflect an impatience on the part of both that is more in keeping with passion than with *fin'amors*, which advocates patience in addition to *mesure*.[31]

Lancelot follows Guenevere's instructions to the letter and arrives outside her window to find her waiting in a white chemise under a short scarlet cloak. As they are kept apart by the iron bars of the window, they can only exchange sweet words and hold hands. Their mutual desire is such that they feel increasingly frustrated at being unable to get closer to each other. Lancelot boasts that if the queen agrees, nothing will prevent him from forcing his way in. She does so, taking the precaution of retiring to bed so that if Lancelot is discovered, her connivance will pass unsuspected. After pulling the bars apart and cutting two fingers to the bone in the process, Lancelot enters the queen's chamber through the window. He kneels down before her as she lies on her bed and venerates her as if she were the reclining figure of a saint. Their love is consummated without delay, and so Lancelot becomes the queen's *drut*. At dawn he sorrowfully goes away, but leaves tell-tale blood-stains on the bed. Meleagant breaks into the room and, on perceiving the blood-stains, accuses Kay of being the queen's paramour. The situation is eventually resolved by Lancelot's equivocal oath and the subsequent judicial combat.[32]

If the *sens* of *Le Chevalier de la Charrette* is the glorification of courtly love, this episode should mark the climax of the romance, and the behaviour

[30] 4501-32.
[31] See M. Lazar, op. cit., p. 32, etc.
[32] 4559-5043.

of the two characters should command the author's approval. But is this the case ? As several scholars have pointed out,[33] the episode has many points in common with one in *Le Roman de Tristan*, in which the lovers are betrayed by blood-stains left by Tristan in Isolt's bed and on the floor between it and his own as he leapt between them to avoid the flour scattered by Frocin.[34] The similarity is so great that it must have been intended by Chrétien and been obvious to the literary public of his day. Chrétien's opinion of Tristan and Isolt's conduct is highly critical in *Cligés* and elsewhere, for he considered that their love was unreasonable, that it brought shame on them and led them to commit *mainte folie*.[35] It seems to me that Chrétien's attitude to Guenevere and Lancelot's night of love is the same and that his purpose in modelling it so closely on the Tristan episode is to underline his disapproval. In spite of their discretion in making the arrangements, the assignation is basically a foolhardy venture in view of Kay's presence, which places them both in considerable danger. As their passion and their frustration at being kept apart grow, so they disregard discretion and proceed with improper haste and inadequate precautions. Passion has made them lose sight of *raison* and *mesure*, and neither is behaving as Chrétien imagines a courtly lover should, though their intimacy brings them unsurpassed *joie*.[36] The adoration of the *dompna* is described without comment, but Chrétien includes the significant remark that Lancelot's love for Guenevere is 100,000 times greater than hers for him,[37] confirming each's attitude towards the other's reported death and casting doubt on the depth of Guenevere's feeling for her knight. This night of love is not *druerie* in its ideal form. It is a further episode which shows Guenevere and Lancelot's shortcomings in the art of courtly love as understood by Chrétien, and in no way marks the climax of the romance.

Shortly after Guenevere's return with Gawain to Arthur's court, a great tournament is organized by the Ladies of Pomelegoi and Noauz, which the queen consents to grace with her presence.[38] When Lancelot, now a prisoner under the guard of Meleagant's seneschal, learns this news, he persuades his captor's wife to let him attend it incognito. The tournament illustrates once more the *desmesure* of the two main characters. Lancelot is submissive to excess, allowing himself to be humiliated and mocked by obeying the queen's command to behave most contemptibly. Guenevere's initial purpose in demanding this behaviour of him can be justified on the grounds

[33] Most recently Professor H. Newstead, in her article entitled " The Equivocal Oath in the Tristan Legend ", *Mélanges offerts à Rita Lejeune*, Vol. II, Gembloux, 1969, p. 1082.

[34] Béroul, *The Romance of Tristran*, ed. Ewert, Oxford, 1939, 643-826.

[35] See *Cligés* 3105-24. See also 28-36 of the second of Chrétien's lyrics edited by W. Foerster in his *Kristian von Troyes. Wörterbuch zu seinen sämtlichen Werken*, Halle, 1914, p. 208*. In this passage the opposition between courtly love and Tristan's love for Isolt is clearly indicated.

[36] 4674-9.

[37] 4663.

[38] 5359-6035.

that it permits her to confirm the unknown knight's identity, but she persists long after this goal has been achieved, instructing him to do his worst at the beginning of the second day. She thus inflicts unnecessary humiliation on her lover by making him appear a coward in public with no other motive than the satisfaction of exercising her authority over him. This raises the whole problem of the right of a *dompna* to endanger her lover's reputation as a knight needlessly. My guess is that in the social context of twelfth-century aristocratic and chivalrous society, which laid such store on personal reputation, Chrétien does not think that she has that right. Instead of carrying out her duty as a *dompna* to help Lancelot to climb towards the peak of chivalry, Guenevere has reverted to her former coquetry now that she has recovered from her sorrow and remorse.

On his voluntary return to his imprisonment in Gorre to fulfil his promise to the seneschal's wife, Lancelot is walled up alone by an angry Meleagant in an isolated tower.[39] Though Guenevere owes Lancelot so much, she does not raise a finger to find him. It is Bademagu's daughter, to whom Lancelot had rendered a far smaller service earlier in the romance, who does this, who sets him free, nurses him back to health and allows him to return to Arthur's court. There is great rejoicing at his return and no one is happier than the queen. Neither she nor Lancelot show their affection for each other in public, and in Guenevere's case we are told that this is because she has now learnt *raison* and is hiding her feelings, intense though they are, until she and Lancelot are alone.[40] The emphasis that Godefroi de Leigni places on the word *raison* at this point is certainly intended to be an echo of its use in the cart scene, in which it was specifically stated that *raison* had made Lancelot hesitate, a hesitation, of course, that Guenevere's craving for domination over her lover had prevented her from appreciating. She has now learnt to exercise *mesure* as a *dompna* should, and this is illustrated still further. She does nothing to hinder Lancelot during his final combat with Meleagant as she had done at the previous tournament, and so he wins a quick and clear victory.

On the other hand, it is more difficult to decide what change has taken place in Lancelot's attitude towards Guenevere. He remains silent about the queen from the point at which he is walled up in the tower to the end of the romance. Surprisingly, his long lamentation in the tower does not contain a single reference to her nor to his love for her.[41] On his release, we are told that he is happy to be on his way back to Arthur's court,[42] but no word is mentioned about him wanting to see the queen. Is this because Lancelot has now learnt complete discretion ? Maybe, but there is nothing in the text to suggest that he, like Guenevere, is waiting for a tête-à-tête before giving vent to his true feelings. Lancelot's apparent indifference is

[39] 6036 ff.
[40] 6820-53.
[41] 6468-529.
[42] 6708.

not all ; there are two short passages which make me wonder whether, as far as he is concerned, the liaison with the queen is over. The first describes his separation from Bademagu's daughter after she has nursed him back to health.

> La pucele beise et acole,
> puis li dist amïablement :
> " Amie, fet il, seulemant
> a Deu et a vos rant merciz
> de ce que sains sui et gariz.
> Par vos sui de prison estors,
> por ce poez mon cuer, mon cors,
> et mon servise, et mon avoir,
> quant vos pleira, prandre et avoir.
> Tant m'avez fet que vostres sui,
> mes grant piece a que je ne sui
> a la cort Artus mon seignor,
> qui m'a portee grant enor ;
> et g'i avroie assez a feire.
> Or, douce amie deboneire,
> par amors si vos prieroie
> congié d'aler, et g'i iroie,
> s'il vos pleisoit, molt volantiers.
> —Lancelot, biax dolz amis chiers,
> fet la pucele, jel vuel bien ;
> que vostre enor et vostre bien
> vuel je par tot et ci et la."
> Un merveilleus cheval qu'ele a,
> le meillor c'onques veïst nus,
> li done cele, et cil saut sus,
> qu'as estriés congié n'an rova :
> ne sot mot quant sus se trova.
> Lors a Deu qui onques ne mant
> s'antrecomandent boenemant.   (6678-6706).

Here Lancelot declares himself Bademagu's daughter's liege-man in the terms of the feudal oath of homage, and then asks her permission to proceed to Arthur's court to complete his business. The lady's reply is in sharp contrast to any that Guenevere has made, and it contains no thought of dominance. Gladly welcoming Lancelot's *service d'amour*, she tells him that her only concern is his *enor* and *bien*, wherever he is, and she grants his request to return to Arthur's court without reservation. This exchange suggests a *service d'amour* in which there are reciprocal duties, similar to feudal vassalage, and in which the submission of the knight to the lady is not unreasoned and absolute, as Lancelot's was to Guenevere for so long. Some may object that it is no more than courtly gallantry on the part of both characters, but later, when describing his imprisonment to Arthur, Lancelot adds, when he has no need to, that he still would have been in the tower,

> se ne fust une moie amie,
> une pucele cui ge fis
> un petit servise jadis.

> Cele por assez petit don
> m'a rendu large guerredon :
> grant enor m'a feite, et grant bien.   (6876-6881)

Is it possible that Bademagu's daughter is now Lancelot's *dompna* ? It is known for courtly liaisons to end when the lover's patience with his lady runs out, as for example in one of Conon de Béthune's poems,[43] and I feel that it is not impossible for this to have happened in *Le Chevalier de la Charrette*. What more satisfactory explanation is there of the silence about Lancelot's feelings for Guenevere during the last thousand lines of the romance ? The evidence is perhaps inconclusive, and so two interpretations of the ending are possible : either Guenevere and Lancelot's liaison continues at Arthur's court under conditions of total discretion and more give and take, or Lancelot has decided to bring it to an end. If either of these interpretations happens to be correct, I think that in this romance Chrétien is trying to do two things : he is showing how Guenevere and Lancelot have fallen short of the *fin'amors* ideal as he and perhaps Marie de Champagne conceive it, and also how certain aspects of the *dompna*/lover relationship as described in Provençal lyric poetry, particularly its introspection, are detrimental to a knight, who, unlike a *troubadour*, is essentially a man of action concerned with the world around him.[44] Guenevere, against whom the more serious criticism is levelled, is too tyrannical and self-centred, not above making a game of love ; she makes excessive demands on Lancelot, failing to reward him adequately in return, and when she actually does so, she is lacking in self-control. Lancelot is over-absorbed in the physical image of his lady and too submissive to her commands, especially when these are palpably exorbitant. Both characters lack the basic discipline made up of *mesure* and *raison* which Chrétien seems to consider inherent to courtly love in a chivalrous society ; it is only at the end of the romance that they have learnt to develop it. If I am right, *Le Chevalier de la Charrette* is not as different in outlook from Chrétien's other romances as has been supposed. Just as *Erec et Enide* and *Le Chevalier au Lion* show how a knight and his wife must find a happy balance between chivalric and matrimonial obligations and that to do so they must apply *mesure* and *raison*, so *Le Chevalier de la Charrette* illustrates how these same qualities are equally essential to a successful extra-marital relationship between a knight and a lady. The *service d'amour* advocated by Chrétien in this romance is one composed of reciprocal duties between the knight and his lady, similar to the allegiance of a vassal to his lord, and not one in which the lover obeys his *dompna's* every whim, while receiving little in return.[45]

[43] See *Les Chansons de Conon de Béthune*, ed. A. Wallensköld, Paris, 1921, IX.

[44] It is possible that the transposition from a lyric to a narrative genre, in which action is essential, is, to some extent, responsible for this change. The opposition can be seen on Chrétien's own work, for in the highly introspective first poem edited by Foerster (op. cit., p. 205*), we are told how love demands of the lover that he abandon *raison* and *mesure*.

[45] My conclusion is diametrically opposed to P. Jonin's in his article " Le Vasselage de Lancelot dans le *Conte de la Charrette* ", *Moyen Âge*, LVIII (1952), 281-98.

What has led literary historians astray in interpreting *Le Chevalier de la Charrette*, it seems to me, has been Marie de Champagne's alleged pronouncement in Andreas Capellanus's *De Amore* on the impossibility of true love in marriage.[46] Since Chrétien states that it was Marie who provided him with the *matière* and *sens* of the romance, literary historians have concluded that its *sens* must be the glorification of extra-marital love. But if Marie's pronouncements as contained in *De Amore* are relevant to the romance, and opinion is now divided on this score,[47] it is important to take into consideration those which criticize the behaviour of lovers as well as the one cited above. For Marie, a lady could make excessive demands on her lover and also she had the duty to return a love equal in intensity to his.[48] Guenevere fails on both counts. Why should Marie not have believed that *raison* and *mesure* were intrinsic to *fin'amors* in the context of a chivalrous society ? Why should she not have asked Chrétien to write a romance showing the pitfalls that could trap a knight and his lady if they failed to cultivate these qualities ? I see no reason at all why she should not have done so. Therefore, it seems to me, the interpretation of the *sens* of *Le Chevalier de la Charrette* that I have proposed is equally feasible, whether Chrétien's statement about Marie de Champagne's instructions to him is to be taken at its face value or not.

A. H. DIVERRES

Aberdeen

[46] " Dicimus enim et stabilito tenore firmamus, amorem non posse suas inter duos iugales extendere vires ". (Andrea Capellano, *Trattato d'amore*, ed. S. Battaglia, Roma, 1947, pp. 178-80. The editor has reproduced Trojel's Latin text.)

[47] The view that criticism of the *Charrette* has been distorted by the ideas of *De Amore* has been expressed by J. Rychner in his article entitled " Le Prologue du *Chevalier de la Charrette* ", *Mélanges offerts à Rita Lejeune*, Vol. II, pp. 1121-35.

[48] " Hunc vero articulum Campaniae comitissa suo taliter explicavit iudicio. Ait enim, quod talis domina nimis in suo fuit mandato severa, quae ipsum non erubuit iniqua sententia supprimere, qui penitus se illius subiugavit arbitrio, et cui spem sui porrexit amoris, quum eum sibi sponsione ligavit, quam nulli probae feminae licit sine causa frustrare " (Andrea Capellano, op. cit., p. 314).

" Miles quidam dominam suam immoderate amabat et eius plenarie fruebatur amplexu, ipsa tamen eum dilectione mutua non amabat. Hic ab ea divertere quaerit, mulier vero ipsum in pristino retinere cupiens statu eiusdem voluntati contradicit.

Huic negotio tale dedit comitissa responsum : Improba nempe satis intentio mulieris iudicatur, quae amari quaerit et ipsa recusat amare. Stultum est enim, aliquem illud ab aliis non reverenter exigere, quod ipse aliis penitus denegat exhibere " (p. 318).

III

PROFANITY AND ITS PURPOSE
IN CHRÉTIEN'S *CLIGÉS* AND *LANCELOT*

The realisation of what Chrétien de Troyes is doing in substantial parts of his *Cligés* and *Lancelot* might move the modern reader to level against him a charge of wilful blasphemy. That no such accusation has, so far as I am aware, been made is due perhaps as much to the common view of Chrétien as an eminently moral, even devout, man as to the circumspection of the critics. His honest reputation may well have played some part in deflecting attention from the remarkable acts of irreverence that he has surreptitiously perpetrated in these two romances—so surreptitiously, indeed, that one might wonder if his contemporary public were always conscious of just what was happening. But when they were, would they have raised the cry of " Blasphemy " ?

I cannot here explore the twelfth-century conception of blasphemy or the Church's attitude towards it. It is reasonable, though, to assume that, despite a certain libertinism to be discerned in courtly and literary circles, Chrétien would not deliberately set out to offend either ecclesiastical authority or the public for whom he worked. So it is more prudent to speak of irreverence or even profanity than of blasphemy ; and there is abundant evidence that this was condoned by the medieval layman, while among the writers it had almost the status of a recognised literary device. But of course there are degrees of irreverence.

The Church, its ministers, institutions and rites were always vulnerable to ridicule, a fact that was exploited to the full by the poets of the *Roman de Renart,* say, or the fabliaux, who had much gross fun at their expense. There was little harm in this or even, given its humorous context, in Aucassin's fervent desire for Hell provided his sweet Nicolette be there—although the aim might here be thought rather nearer to the heart of the Christian faith. If we raise our eyebrows higher at Gottfried von Strassburg's notorious reference to Christ's pliancy in abetting dishonest acts, this can perhaps be passed off as irony and Gottfried's character remain untarnished.

Courtly love was a theme particularly apt to attract more or less daring embellishment. The romance of *Guillaume de Dole,* for instance, offers a picture of knights and ladies philandering in tents pitched in a smiling countryside :

> Il ne pensent pas a lor ames ;
> Si n'i ont cloches ne moustiers
> (Qu'il n'en est mie granz mestiers),
> Ne chapelains fors les oiseaus.[1]

---

[1] *Le Roman de la Rose ou de Guillaume de Dole,* ed. G. Servois, Paris (S.a.t.fr.), 1893, ll. 224-7.

Latin writings were certainly no less reticent than the vernacular texts. However innocent the intention, there is surely more than a touch of irreverence about the delicious " Si linguis angelicis . . .", with its very earthly love expressed through the phraseology of the liturgy. Take the stanza so transparently modelled on the *Ave Maria* :

> Ave, formosissima gemma preciosa !
> ave decus virginum, virgo gloriosa !
> ave lumen luminum, ave mundi rosa,
> Blanziflôr et Helena, Venus generosa !²

But if here a plea for leniency may be advanced, there can be no doubt of the profanity of that outrageous burlesque of Church assemblies, the *Council of Remiremont*.³ It is convened under the presidency of a female cardinal to debate the relative merits as lovers of knights and clerics. Ovid is read " quasi evangelium " ; and the judgment is given that those who henceforth love knights in preference to ecclesiastics will be excommunicated.

Among the Latin writings we must not forget a strange episode in the *De amore* of Andreas Capellanus, Chrétien's contemporary and, one assumes, his acquaintance at Troyes. I mean the description of the company of dead women and their lovers led by the God of Love, and the portrayal of the otherworld where they dwell in greater or lesser bliss according to their amorous deserts.⁴ The whole account is clearly patterned on Christian eschatological notions as embodied in texts such as the *Vision of St Paul* (one of the women is even granted respite from her pains at the instance of the narrator) ; and the enumeration by the God of Love of his twelve commandments merely extends the irreverence. Incidentally, the French *Lai du trot*,⁵ which is based on Andreas' story, omits the more obviously parodic sections.

It is a commonplace of troubadour poetry that in the expression of profane love the terminology of divine love often found a home, and vice versa. Could this have played some part in encouraging a parodic element when the love situation is treated in this or that romance ? It would be unwise to take the argument of cause and effect too far ; but the possibility may be worth considering, particularly in connection with Chrétien's romances. For we know that he practised the courtly lyric himself. And in one of his two surviving poems there is a trace of religious phraseology :

> S'Amors por essaucier sa loi
> viaut ses anemis convertir,
> de sans li vient, si con je croi,
> qu'as suens ne puet ele faillir.⁶

---

² See Peter Dronke, who edits the poem, in *Medieval Latin and the Rise of European Love-Lyric* (Oxford, 1965) I, 318 ff. Dronke is doubtless right in arguing against conscious blasphemy.

³ Ed. Horst Kusch, *Einführung in das lateinische Mittelalter* (Berlin, 1957), I, 354-67.

⁴ Ed. Amadeu Pagès, Castelló de la Plana, 1930, pp. 53 ff.

⁵ Ed. E. Margaret Grimes in *Romanic Review* XXVI (1935), 313-21.

⁶ Ed. W. Foerster in *Kristian von Troyes, Wörterbuch*, Halle, 1914, p. 207*.

But if there is a link between such a conceit as this and the extreme ir-reverence I shall point to in his romances, it is frail indeed.

Before considering these romances, we may recall one other French text, the thirteenth-century fabliau *Saint Pierre et le jongleur*. The poor minstrel dies in sin and is carried off to Hell, where even Lucifer's heart is touched by his wretched condition, and he is left in charge of the infernal cauldron and all the damned when the devils leave to pursue their forays on earth. A dignified old gentleman enters the nether realm and induces him, without much difficulty, to stake the souls in a dice game. St Peter, for the intruder was no less a personage, makes coup after coup until he is able to lead the entire company of rejoicing souls back with him to Paradise. Now as I have shown elsewhere,[7] the basic theme of this tale parodies the popular accounts of Christ's Harrowing of Hell. Even the most solemn moments of the Christian story were not immune in the Middle Ages from such irreverent, parodic treatment.

This is not the kind of thing, however, that we would expect from Chrétien, even if we have little faith in the arguments of those who would make of him a pious allegorist. He was, we are.bound to feel, a man of conventionally upright views, stressing in particular the orthodox line on love (no adulterous liaisons for him, whether in the Provençal style or after the fashion of Tristan), and insisting on the religious element in the education of a young man bent on chivalry. Yet at the same time there is a certain disingenuousness about most of his works bred not from malice or deceit but from an ability to stand at a critical distance from his characters and their problems. Chrétien is one of the most coolly intelligent of French writers and endowed moreover with an extremely fine-grained sense of humour. As a result, I believe that most of his work has an ambivalent quality : he is inclined to compose tongue-in-cheek, inviting us to take his story seriously if we wish, but hinting that it would be more fun if we would share the secret joke he is playing on his heroes and heroines.

In an excellent recent study, Peter Haidu comes to similar conclusions.[8] He sees in particular an ironical intention informing many of the situations in *Cligés*. This is doubtless so ; and in one important instance I think he could have gone a good deal deeper in his examination of the " aesthetic distance " between author and characters or events. I refer to the episode of Fénice's feigned death.

It will be remembered that, despite the mutual love of Cligés and Fénice, the girl has been forced to marry Cligés' uncle, the Emperor of Greece and Constantinople. Her virginity is nevertheless spared through the administra-tion to the Emperor of a potion concocted by her witch of a nurse, Thessala. Cligés proposes an elopement to Brittany ; but Fénice fears they would earn the reputation of Tristan and Iseut ; and she misquotes St Paul to the

[7] " The Element of Parody in *Saint Pierre et le jongleur* ", *French Studies* IX (1955), 60-3.

[8] *Aesthetic Distance in Chrétien de Troyes : Irony and Comedy in " Cligés " and " Perceval "*, Genève, 1968.

effect that those who will not live chaste should act with such caution as to avoid public reproach. Her plan is to feign death, so that Cligés will be able to rescue her from the tomb and carry her off to some hidden retreat. To this end Thessala will prepare another of her potions, whilst Jehan, a serf of Cligés', will construct a sepulchre and place a secret tower of his own at the lovers' disposal. The plan is almost brought to grief by the meddlesome interference of three physicians from Salerno, who suspect a trick and try to revive Fénice by torturing her. But in the end it is carried through, and the lovers find their happiness in Jehan's splendid tower and a delightful adjoining garden.

The case I wish to put is that Chrétien has modelled the whole of this episode of shammed death and revival on the account, probably the scriptural account, of Christ's Passion and Resurrection. To begin with, though he tells us that the maiden's name was Fénice because of the unrivalled beauty of the phoenix, others have pointed out that the bird that rose from its ashes was also used in the Middle Ages as a symbol of resurrection. I would go further and suggest that Chrétien had in mind Christ's own rising from the dead, which is the allegory supplied by the medieval bestiaries. Let us, then, look at the episode in more detail.

At the beginning of Fénice's pretended illness, a curious equation is made between Cligés and God. When the empress says that one alone has the power of life or death over her, the bystanders think she refers to God. But Chrétien makes it plain :

. . . ele n'antant s'a Cligés non :
C'est ses Dex qui la puet garir
Et qui la puet feire morir.   (5644-6)[9]

This sets the tone for what follows.

Significant, I think, are certain indications of time, as when all agree that Fénice cannot go beyond the ninth hour before yielding up the ghost, and it is then that she is given Thessala's potion to drink. (We recall the hour of Christ's death, as well as the vinegar in the sponge.) At once the draught has its effect, and all cry aloud thinking her dead. They lament the loss of " la meillor chose et la plus sainte " (5728) ; and when the three physicians arrive on the scene, they are told that God had illumined the world with a radiance and light that death has now extinguished, and in one person death has carried off more goodness than it has left behind on earth (5770-80). At this point one reflects that such hyperbole is hardly apt when applied to a woman who is duping her wedded husband, whereas of course it is not only appropriate but commonly used with reference to Christ. In particular, much play is made on the idea of Christ the light of the world in that section of the apocryphal *Gospel of Nicodemus* which relates the Harrowing of Hell[10] and which, as we shall see, was not unknown to Chrétien.

[9] I quote from the edition by A. Micha, Paris (C.f.m.â), 1957.

[10] Ed. C. Tischendorf, *Evangelia apocrypha*, Leipzig, 1853. Translation by M. R. James, *The Apocryphal New Testament*, Oxford, 1924, pp. 94 ff.

The suspicious physicians get to work. In order to expose Fénice's pretence, they first scourge her savagely with leather thongs (5900-11), but to no effect. Then they boil lead, which they pour onto her hands so that the palms are quite pierced (5924-5). (The parallels with the Crucifixion are too obvious to need comment.) And when we are told that over a thousand women watch Fénice's ordeal through a small opening in the palace door (5934-41), we think of the scriptural account (for instance in *Matthew* XXVII.55) of the many women who beheld the Crucifixion from afar. They see Fénice's *martire*—"torment", or more technically "martyrdom"— and the word is later repeated (5941, 5972).

When the women have defenestrated the physicians, Thessala anoints Félice's wounds with a very precious ointment, and the women wrap the body in a white cloth (5980-9). We are specifically told that they leave the face uncovered; and the point could have been made in deliberate contrast with the use of the napkin in Christ's entombment, as reported both in *John* XX.7 and in the *Gospel of Nicodemus*. That night is spent in lamentations.

Next day Jehan is ordered by the Emperor to construct a tomb. But he says (and of course we are at once reminded of Joseph of Arimathaea) that he has already prepared a finely hewn sepulchre, which he had intended for a holy body or relic; but let the Empress be laid there, for she is "molt sainte chose" (6004-12).

Fénice's body is taken for burial; but its bearers fall in a swoon (6069; cf. *Matthew* XXVIII.4), so that Jehan is able to make his final adjustments unseen. He closes and seals the sepulchre with care, and for no clear reason a guard is set (6074, 6081). Again we recall a verse of *Matthew* (XXVII.66): "Illi autem abeuntes, munierunt sepulcrum, signantes lapidem, cum custodibus."

That night the guards fall asleep (6086-7: they merely report having slept in *Matthew* XXVIII.13); and Cligés comes with Jehan to remove the body. The sepulchre is opened after Cligés has descended from a tree into the cemetery (a reminiscence, perhaps, of the angel's descent to roll back the stone?). And Fénice's body is removed to the tower. There she revives and is restored to health by means of Thessala's ointments and medicaments. And I might add that if one cares to work out the chronology of these events, it appears that the "resurrection" took place during the night preceding the third day. Moreover, Fénice, though not caught up to Heaven, is reunited with her lover (who had earlier been equated with the deity) in a veritable paradise on earth.

All these correspondences cannot be explained away as coincidence. Nor would I care to ascribe them to unwitting, involuntary reminiscence by Chrétien of the well-known scriptural events. I am sure he knew what he was about; and so this amounts to a deliberate and quite methodical use for the elaboration of his story of the account of the Crucifixion and Resurrection—parody certainly, even burlesque? The incongruity of it all is startling. Here is a love-situation of which Chrétien surely disapproved, involving moral if not legal adultery (the non-consummation of Fénice's marriage left a legal loophole),[11] with the wife's deceit of her husband acted out in terms of the central Christian mystery. What could Chrétien's purpose have been ?

And what was his purpose in *Lancelot*, composed some time later ? This is a romance entirely devoted to the adulterous pursuit by Lancelot of his liege lord's wife ; and throughout the central section, Chrétien chooses to incorporate what amounts to a diffuse parody of Christ's Harrowing as set out in the *Gospel of Nicodemus*.[12] Let me summarise the relevant parts of *Nicodemus* from the Latin versions that were well known in Chrétien's day.[13]

After Christ left the tomb, many other sepulchres were found to be empty ; and among the resurrected were Simeon's two sons, who made separate depositions about their experience. They had been in Hell with all those who had died from the beginning of the world, when the darkness was dispelled by a great light. The prophets announce that this heralds the coming of the Son of God for their deliverance.

While all the saints rejoice at the news, Satan the prince of Hell bids Inferus prepare to receive Jesus ; but Inferus is alarmed, fearing that he has come to deprive Hell of its dead. The devils' dispute is interrupted by a thunderous voice commanding that they remove the gates so that the King of Glory may come in. Inferus orders Satan out to meet the intruder ; but after a further summons, the gates and their bars are shattered, and Christ enters in majesty. Inferus and Death and their legions admit defeat. Christ tramples upon Death, delivers Satan into the keeping of Inferus, and draws the exulting souls of the righteous into his glory.

To return now to Chrétien, Lancelot has pursued his search for the abducted Guenevere to the bounds of the mysterious land of Gorre, whence no traveller returns (and in which most scholars recognise some Celtic other-world in thin disguise). For part of the way he has ridden in a shameful tumbril—a re-enactment of Christ's journey to Calvary ?[14] In any case, when he enters a cemetery full of empty tombs, we are surely entitled to recall the happenings after the Crucifixion. The finest tomb bears an inscription referring to the slab that covers it :

" Cil qui levera

[11] See Erich Köhler, *Ideal und Wirklichkeit in der höfischen Epik* (*ZRP* Beiheft 97), Tübingen, 1956, p. 162 n. 1.

[12] While this paper was in preparation I found the same suggestion briefly advanced by A. L. Morton in *The Matter of Britain* (London, 1966), pp. 21-2. More recently Professor David C. Fowler reached a similar conclusion in a paper, " Love in Chrétien's Lancelot ", delivered to the Ninth International Arthurian Congress in Cardiff on 8th August, 1969. Others, especially Köhler (op. cit., pp. 124-6), have noticed parallels to the Harrowing tradition in general.

[13] Surviving vernacular versions date from the early thirteenth century, including one by a poet named Chrétien who may have hailed from Champagne, but is not to be identified with the author of *Lancelot*.

[14] Both Morton and Fowler believe so ; and though the evidence is less than con-clusive, the possibility cannot be dismissed.

> cele lanme seus par son cors
> gitera ces et celes fors
> qui sont an la terre an prison,
> don n'ist ne clers ne gentix hon
> des l'ore qu'il i est antrez ;
> n'ancors n'en est nus retornez :
> les estranges prisons retienent ;
> et cil del pais vont et vienent
> et anz et fors a lor pleisir."
>
> $(1900-9)^{15}$

Lancelot raises the slab without effort and pursues his journey.

He has now entered the hostile realm ; and some captives he meets tell him that there is no escape from the land (which is envisaged as one vast prison) until such time as one of them manages to leave, when all will be free to go without hindrance. The inhabitants are " gent sarradine / qui peior que Sarrazin sont " (2134-5).

Word of Lancelot's arrival soon spreads among the captives, and an enemy squire reports :

> " Ce dïent an cest païs tuit
> que il les deliverra toz
> et metra les noz au desoz."
>
> (2300-2)

With some companions he is briefly shut in a castle; but coming to a gate, they assault it and break the bar (2356-60) to emerge into a place where the captives are in revolt against their oppressors. Lancelot enters the fray with predictable success, and the captives ask who is this knight. Their joy knows no bounds when they are told :

> " Seignor, ce est cil
> qui nos gitera toz d'essil
> et de la grant maleürté
> ou nos avons lonc tans esté ;
> se li devons grant enor feire
> quant, por nos fors de prison treire,
> a tant perilleus leus passez . . ."
>
> (2413-9)

Chrétien now leaves for a time the scheme of the *Gospel of Nicodemus* to describe Lancelot's passage of the sword bridge. It may be that for this feature as for many others in the romance there is a remote Celtic source. But details of Chrétien's account leave us in very little doubt that he had in mind the testing bridge of Hell as described in the *Vision of St Paul*, *St Patrick's Purgatory*, or some other well-known pious legend. Not only does it span a torrent as grim and black " con se fust li fluns au deable " (3012), but it is razor-sharp and may be crossed only by a true believer. Lancelot has no fear :

> " Mes j'ai tel foi et tel creance
> an Deu qu'il me garra par tot."
>
> (3084-5)

---

[15] Ed. Mario Roques, Paris (C.f.m.â.), 1958.

So Chrétien is still thinking in eschatological terms; and in describing Lancelot's painful crossing of the bridge he prepares the way for a fresh injection of *Nicodemus* material. For from this point on, considerable stress is laid on the fact that the heroic deliverer is sorely wounded in his hands and feet.

After his ordeal he comes to the castle of King Bademagu, father of Guenevere's abductor Meleagant. From a window the king and his son have witnessed " le plus grant hardemant / qui onques fust mes nes pansez " (3192-3); and Bademagu is prepared to receive Lancelot into his castle. But his son shows only hostility; and there follows a heated dispute reminiscent of the quarrel between Satan and Inferus at the coming of Christ, though the arguments and motives are made to conform, of course, to the romance situation.

Eventually Bademagu goes out to meet Lancelot, honouring him for the unique courage of his feat : no other such perilous undertaking has ever been or will ever be achieved. He will see to the healing of his wounds, he says. And then, as if to leave no doubt as to the parallel he is drawing, Chrétien puts these very incongruous words into Bademagu's mouth :

> " De l'oignemant as trois Maries
> et de meillor, s'an le trovoit,
> vos doñrai ge . . ."
> (3358-60)

A duel is arranged between Lancelot and Meleagant ; and all the captives flock together to watch it as if they were assembling for church on a feast day. The captive maidens from Arthur's court had fasted and gone barefoot for three days (surely a covert allusion to the three days of Easter)

> por ce que Dex force et vertu
> donast contre son aversaire
> au chevalier, qui devoit faire
> la bataille por les cheitis
> (3528-31)

We notice that although the real matter at issue between these two is the possession of Guenevere, it is the broader concern that is given prominence here, plainly by analogy with the Harrowing. And again we are told that

> Li prison et les prisonieres
> trestuit por lor seignor prioient,
> qu'an Deu et an lui se fioient
> de secors et de delivrance.
> (3580-3)

Their prayers are answered, Meleagant is worsted in the duel, and Lancelot thus earns the queen's release. Once more we are reminded that if one goes, all are free to leave. So the captives' joy knows no bounds : they throng round Lancelot, welcoming him as their predestined saviour, each one struggling to touch him ; and for those who succeed there is no greater bliss (3906-20). And all do in the end return to Arthur's court.

The case for a parodic treatment of the Christian story seems as incontestable here as in *Cligés*. But in neither instance do I suggest that the parody is in itself humorous. Certainly we have cause to smile as we reflect that Lancelot, who elsewhere in the romance is abject almost to the point of imbecility in his devotion to Guenevere, nevertheless appears to acquire through the parody and his role of predestined saviour an aura of near-divinity. Yet when we consider these elements apart from the burlesque which I take to underlie the rest of the romance, they have nothing of the comic about them. Again, it is rather the incongruity that strikes us.

We find Chrétien once more using an otherworld motif in his unfinished burlesque romance of Gauvain (which is what I hold the second part of the Conte du Graal to be). Here too it is associated with the hero's sentimental involvements, since the recurrent theme in his adventures is his fatal weakness for the fair sex. On the other hand, I see no hint of irreverence or Christian parody in the Château des Merveilles episode, which embodies the otherworld material.

Now I believe that Chrétien's Gauvain (if I may call it that) inspired at least two other short burlesque romances in which Arthur's nephew plays the chief part.[16] And in one of these we do find the profane and parodic use of pious texts. It is La Mule sans frein (also known as the Demoiselle à la mule) ;[17] and in the course of a prologue inspired by Chrétien's introduction to his Erec, the author names himself as Paien de Maisières. This is evidently a play on the elements of " Chrétien de Troyes " ; but while one cannot dismiss the possibility that this is Chrétien himself working under a pseudonym, it is safer for the present to assume that we are dealing with a pupil, perhaps, or at least an admirer of the poet of Troyes. In any case, he was well conversant with Chrétien's work and techniques.

The story tells of how first Kay and then Gauvain set out in search of a bridle mislaid by the damsel of the alternative title. They ride on her mule, which leads them through a forest peopled by wild beasts and then into a deep, dark valley. The fire-breathing serpents and other creatures lurking there are fearsome enough, but even worse is the terrible stench of the place ; and a further torment is the bitter, eternal cold as well as the biting winds that blow. The travellers emerge into a fair and flowery meadow, where a clear spring provides refreshment. But beyond this is a rushing, black river spanned by an iron bridge of no more than a hand's breadth. The poet explains that this is " li fluns au deable " (398), and one seems to see nothing but demons in it. The sight is too much for Kay ; but when Gauvain comes there, he commends himself to God and rides across the bridge, which sags frighteningly as he goes.

The borrowing from eschatological legend is transparent ; and again, as I have said, it is worked into a general burlesque context. The valley belongs

[16] See my articles : " Paien de Maisières—A Joke That Went Wrong ", FMLS II (1966), 192-6 ; and " Burlesque Tradition and Sir Gawain and the Green Knight ", FMLS IV (1968), 125-45.

[17] Ed. R. T. Hill (Baltimore, 1911) and by B. Orlowski (Paris, 1911). A new edition by Professor R. C. Johnston and myself is in preparation. We shall discuss the question of authorship in our Introduction.

to the infernal regions, with its typical features of darkness, vermin, over-powering stench, extreme cold and wind. The meadow and fountain be-yond recall accounts of the Earthly Paradise, normally reached by the traveller after Hell is passed ; but with the bridge we are back to the places of torment and the testing bridge over the infernal river that we encountered in *Lancelot*. The pleasant region has merely been misplaced. The details are still too commonplace for us to identify a particular source, but the visions of St Paul and Tundal, and the legend of St Patrick's Purgatory spring to mind.

If I am right in my belief that *La Mule sans frein* was a direct source for the Middle English *Sir Gawain and the Green Knight*[18] and that this French account of the infernal valley inspired Gawain's wintry journey on his way to the Green Knight's dwelling, it is interesting to find that the Englishman has stripped away all the eschatological connotations, including the river and its testing bridge. He could scarcely have failed to recognise them for what they are. So it may be that he found more pleasure in the description of nature than of diabolic device. Or perhaps (and this is quite likely) he disapproved the irreverence implicit in the French narrative. Along with the reticence shown, as I remarked, by the author of the *Lai du trot*, this might be construed as showing that not all medieval writers of romance were equally happy to indulge in the profane exploitation of themes from devout writings.

There is another feature of *La Mule sans frein* that I should like to mention. It occurs when Gauvain has achieved his quest, in the course of which he has slain some ferocious beasts that had kept the inhabitants of a castle cowering in cellars and crypts. They joyfully emerge ; and Gauvain is told :

> " . . . Or dïent en lor langage :
> Dieus les a par vos delivrez,
> Et de toz biens enluminez
> La gent qui en tenebre estoient.
> Si grant joie ont de ce qu'il voient
> qu'il ne püent graingnor avoir."

(1030-5)

Here we catch echoes of Zacharias' prophecy in *Luke* I.79 that Christ will come to give light to them that sit in darkness ; and we think of *Isaiah* IX.2 : " Populus, qui ambulabat in tenebris, vidit lucem magnam." But we remember too that such phraseology as this is found in the *Gospel of Nicodemus* and is typical of the accounts of Christ's spoliation of Hell. The pseudo-Paien de Maisières is plainly thinking of Gauvain's somewhat fortu-itous salvation of the castle's inhabitants in terms of the Harrowing. He has learnt well from his master.

It seems, then, that after Chrétien the insertion of this kind of profane cross-reference to pious texts in the course of tales of courtly adventure was recognised as a legitimate literary device. Sometimes it appears innocent

[18] See my article in *FMLS* IV (1968), 125-45.

enough. The use of the testing bridge does not shock in a genre where perilous passages of one kind or another abound ; and indeed we find it reappearing in a number of works, including the Second Continuation of the *Perceval, Perlesvaus*, the prose *Lancelot*, and the Dutch romance of *Walewein*. Certainly it is much indebted to the infernal bridge of Christian legend, whatever one's views may be on Celtic prototypes ; but it would be unfair to brand as impiety the purloining of a purely mechanical contraption so suitable for trying the mettle of venturesome knights.

The parodic treatments of Crucifixion and Harrowing must, though, give real food for thought. And again the question arises as to whether deliberate blasphemy is conceivable. I take it that blasphemy would be present if there were in these texts some intention to bring the Christian story into ridicule by reducing its events to the level of a dubious adventure tale. But this, surely, was never in the authors' minds. In so far as any ridicule was intended, it must have been aimed at the hero (or heroine in the case of Fénice), who is bound to suffer in the comparison that is offered with Christ—unless, of course, one feels that the analogy makes Fénice's endurance seem more admirable and serves to magnify the achievements of Lancelot and Gauvain. In either case, the authors would not be conscious of doing anything to offend the susceptibilities of their public.

So now we have to decide whether there is in fact any intention to ridicule the characters, or whether they were really being paid a rather oblique compliment. This cannot be settled by looking at the particular episodes in isolation : they have each to be seen against the background of the whole romance, and here opinions may well differ. In the case of *Lancelot* and *La Mule sans frein* I would plead for an underlying burlesque intention. Throughout his adventures Lancelot is for me a mock-heroic figure. He stumbles, like Gauvain in Chrétien's last romance, from one embarrassment into another. And most of them stem not from external circumstances but from his own abject passion for the queen, which reduces him to a quite pitiful state. He almost throws himself out of a window, suffers agonies of conscience having agreed to go to bed with a charming hostess, is so rapt in his reveries that he fails to hear a challenge and comes to in the cold waters of a ford ; he fights Meleagant with his back turned so as not to take his eyes off Guenevere. . . Need I go on ? Aucassin was not more besotted by love than was Lancelot, and the effect is different only in degree. And so, rather than impute to Chrétien an inconsistency in his portrayal, I take the episodes under discussion to have their place in the total burlesque design. The same applies to *La Mule sans frein*, where Gauvain rides to meet his destiny on the eponymous mule, has to make a well-timed leap into a spinning castle, and there undergo a beheading test and fight a stout tussle with a knight who had previously been run through the body.

The case of *Cligés* is less obvious. But here, as in *Lancelot*, Chrétien is illustrating the exaggerations to which a wrongly based love can lead. He carries the lovers headlong on, but at the same time invites us to withhold our full sympathy. Three times he makes Fénice express her horror of being classed with Iseut ; but she goes in the end one better than even Tristan's *amie*. So I would suggest that in the feigned death episode there is at least a touch of burlesque ; and our amused disapproval is not lessened by the thought that if this is Fénice's Passion, it is a very private and selfish one, and without any redemptive value beyond herself and Cligés.

If I am right, one might well ask if some of this might not be lost on the public of the day. Indeed it might. But that, I believe, was part of Chrétien's genius. He deliberately composed at least the majority of his romances in such a fashion that his public could take them in one of two ways, as I suggested earlier : either with straight faces, or with a grain or two of his own mocking humour. " Here is my story of Lancelot ", he might say. " What a buffoon he is—or what an example to all courtly lovers ! And here is Fénice. Just see what deceits she could practise to get by an unwanted husband. Or, if you prefer, how nearly she illustrates Christ's saying that there is no greater love than to lay down one's life for one's friends." Is it too rash to wonder if something of this double vision may not be reflected in his treatment of the loves of Erec, Yvain, even Perceval ? Chrétien was a writer of greater subtlety than is always recognised. Moreover, he was composing for a fairly heterogeneous public of both sexes, and we should not assume uniformity in either tastes or intelligence or in the degree to which individuals would associate themselves with his characters.

His displays of irreverence, then, were far from gratuitous. They supplied a purposeful element of incongruity in his romances, designed to advance his burlesque schemes, or at least to set his audience, or those of them who wished, at a critical distance from his characters and their actions. Irreverence, but not blasphemy, was part of his artistic technique, and a very significant part. He may well have invented this particular use of it ; at all events it was recognised and taken over by the poet of *La Mule sans frein*. And it is interesting to reflect that already with the father of Arthurian romance we find a concern to probe its weaknesses in this and other ways. But that is another and wider question. Suffice it now to sound a note of praise for a very sophisticated and truly remarkable artistic personality, a man as daring in his techniques as he was enigmatic in his purposes, a man of aristocratic talent but who as often as not applied that talent, I fancy, to the sly pulling of courtly legs.[19]

D. D. R. OWEN

St Andrews

---

[19] This article is based on a paper read to the Leeds University Medieval Group on 19th May, 1969.

IV

IRONY AND MEDIEVAL ROMANCE [1]

The German Romantics, although wedded to their own form of irony, felt so strong a need to idealise the medieval past that they were strangely reluctant to concede that some of the medieval works they most admired might appeal to them through a kindred ironic spirit. To Ludwig Tieck these works spoke unambiguously : " Die Dichtkunst war kein Kampf gegen etwas, kein Beweis, kein Streit für etwas, sie setzte in schöner Unschuld den Glauben an das voraus, was sie besingen wollte, daher ihre ungesuchte, einfältige Sprache in dieser Zeit." This Romantic attribution to an idealised past of qualities which we moderns lack has persisted into our own century, but is now coming under heavier fire and we are being forced to revise attitudes that we have uncritically inherited from the last century. Not only Lukács (from his Marxist point of view), but other scholars too are aware of the role played by the French Revolution and the Napoleonic Wars in stimulating the Romantic need to turn to an idealised feudalism and to find its unbroken reflection in medieval literature. If we have come to distrust the Romantics' objectivity, we have also grown more critical of the poetic innocence and simplicity which they imputed to medieval literature. In this respect de Boor, who interprets Kalogreant's definition of knighthood as a programmatic view upheld by his author and not as the scathing burlesque which most of us now see in it, is still true to the Romantic conception. Similarly, I doubt whether this observation by so judicious a scholar as Mockenhaupt in 1942 (" Einen Ritter wie Wolfram . . . kann eine ethische Problematik des Kampfes so wenig anfechten, wie eine Infrageziehung des Rittertums selbst ") could be seriously sustained today.

I realise, of course, that we run the same risk as the Romantics and that our sensibility to the note of critical dissent in the past is as much a product of our century's disillusionment as was the Romantics' need to glorify the past a reaction to the historical experiences of their day. But to explain the historical and psychological circumstances which gave birth to a particular approach to literature is not to invalidate that approach as such, so that it is conceivable that both the Romantics' idealising interpretation and· the current awareness of critical dissent correspond to distinct features in the works concerned. If this is so, then it suggests that the feature of irony may have an important part to play in reconciling such discrepancies, in accounting for a literary idealisation of chivalry which does not exclude a

[1] This article was given, in substantially this form, as a lecture at a number of universities in the United States and Canada in 1969. Because I have retained its lecture form I have felt justified in omitting all bibliographical references and acknowledgments. This omission will be made good in a book on this subject which I am now preparing.

realistic awareness of its deficiencies. That master of modern irony, Thomas Mann, described his instrument in terms that are relevant to the medieval problem : " Liebe plus Kritik gleich Ironie ". In their depiction of an ideal chivalry the knightly authors of our romances show their admiration for the potentialities of knighthood, but the masterpieces at least also betray a knowledge of its actual deficiencies, of the discrepancy between what is and what should be. From this discrepancy arises much of the force of medieval irony, which is all the more telling in its invitation to self-examination in that it involves no direct attack on knighthood from without (as in the clerical invective of Heinrich von Melk), but rather a voicing of doubts from within the ranks of chivalry. The audience is therefore led to accept this knightly criticism of knighthood as its own and is induced to undertake its own self-criticism—such creative participation by the audience in the author's intentions is an essential feature of irony.

It would be possible to show the overall importance of irony by a discussion of medieval rhetoric and the various tropes which could be termed *ironia* or associated with it, but this would smack too much of the medieval schoolroom, whilst the practical demonstration of the function of irony in any one work is too complex for the narrow limits of an essay. Instead, I propose to discuss something of the wide scope of irony in the medieval romance by looking at the five types of irony we encounter, proceeding from the simplest and small-scale feature of verbal irony through to the more subtle and sustained artistry of structural irony, illustrating my remarks with examples from a few leading works in German, French and English literature.

We may start with verbal irony as the simplest type because its range is frequently so restricted that the discrepancy between utterance and context is immediately apparent. It is perhaps this frequent absence of long-range implications that explains why it is irony of this nature that occurs before the rise of the romance, in epic poetry where grim warrior humour often has recourse to what we might call " heroic irony " in its battle descriptions. Already in Old High German the *Ludwigslied* describes the hero smiting his foes as " pouring them out a bitter wine " (v. 53 f.), whilst in English the *Battle of Maldon* sees battle ironically as a " reconciliation " between enemies by means of the sword (v. 60), and weapons as a tribute to be paid (v. 46 f.). The knightly encounters of the romance still give ample scope for this kind of ironic understatement. Wolfram is particularly fond of it and describes, for example, Gramoflanz' combat with Parzival in these terms (706, 15 : *sîner vriwendinne künne | leit ouch bî im swache wünne*)—here the irony lies in the ignorance of the two contestants of the link between them (Parzival is related to his opponent's mistress), but also in the nature of the " advantage " which this kinship brings—a rain of swordblows. Closely related to this irony of understatement is that of inversion, where the author says the opposite of what he means or derives his imagery from an incongruous sphere. Indeed, Chrétien and Hartmann use this method so recurrently that their descriptions of combat differ from those in the heroic epic by their overall implication that these encounters might not have been a serious matter of life and death—their constant metaphorical equation of combat with its opposite (love, friendship, playfulness) drastically tones the issue down and places a stylistic barrier between the audience and the harsh reality described. Ironic criticism is implied when Hartmann describes his hero Iwein, the victor over Askalon, as *ein so hövesch man* (v. 1040), for he gives him this apparent praise when denying his knowledge of the details of this combat (for a courtly victor would not have boasted about it by telling others), but carefully adds his comment that Iwein, by seeking to gain his opponent as a trophy, alive or dead, to present to Arthur's court, is taken up with precisely that need for courtly renown that a chivalric hero can afford to ignore, certainly when the cost is another man's life.

A rhetorical play on words can also be used to produce an ironic effect. Chrétien's Cligès takes leave of Fénice with words which could be intrepreted as a conventional farewell or as a concealed declaration of love (v. 4282 f.), just as Gottfried's Riwalin is left to ponder over a similarly ambiguous remark by Blanscheflur (v. 744 ff.), whilst we, the audience, look on in full awareness of what is at stake. In his *Perceval* Chrétien depicts the chance encounter of Gauvain on his wanderings with the young king of Escavalon, who invites the knight to enjoy the amenities of his castle and entrusts him to the care of his sister while he himself continues his hunt. There is dramatic irony in this invitation since the king had sworn enmity to Gauvain, so that presumably, had he been aware of Gauvain's identity, he would have offered him a duel rather than hospitality. But this is reinforced by the ironic ambiguity with which he commends Gauvain to the attentions of his sister, using the verb *aimer* (v. 5735 f.), applicable in Old French both to social and to sexual intercourse. Since we, unlike the king, are aware of Gauvain's identity and of his reputation as a ladykiller, there is a nice verbal irony in this unwitting recommendation which Gauvain and the sister are not slow to follow when they are soon afterwards discovered on the brink of lovemaking.

From an ambiguous play on words it is but a short step to a quotation or proverb employed ironically. Gottfried's Tristan at one stage attempts to justify himself by a recurrent appeal to Ovid's teaching on love, but since this occurs precisely when he is about to fall short of his author's ideal by abandoning the first Isold for the sake of the second this shows up the dubious mentor he has chosen as an excuse for his failure. Wolfram makes use of a proverb well known to his audience when he underlines the folly of his young Valois hero, Parzival, by saying (121, 7 : *ein pris den wir Beier tragen, | muoz ich von Wâleisen sagen : | die sint toerscher denne beiersch her*) and by adding ironically that a man born in both regions would indeed be a paragon of intelligence. This proverbial reputation of the Bavarians establishes a link, disconcerting for Wolfram's Bavarian audience, between themselves and the young hero to whom they may have regarded themselves, up to this point, as comfortably superior.

The same technique is extended, with profounder implications, whenever it is a leading concept of courtly vocabulary which is ironised. Chrétien can eulogise Gauvain, as the representative knight of the Round Table, and a particular hero such as Yvain by means of the honorific *messire*, but when this same title is applied, quite exceptionally, to the evil-tongued Ké we can be sure that this was intended as malicious irony at the senechal's expense. Elsewhere in the same romance the author sings the praise, in highly mannered terms, of a young lady worthy of marriage to a hero, remarking that the God of Love himself would gladly renounce his divinity for her sake (v. 5375 ff.). A pleasant conceit, but one that puts this courtly deity in his place, for he is made to serve here only as a foil to Yvain who, in this scene, remains faithful to his wife and, unlike the divinity, is firm enough to resist such blandishments. Unexpected dimensions are suddenly revealed when Chaucer, in his *Knight's Tale*, has the knight Arcite refer to his beloved as (v. 1922) : *my sweete foo, myn Emelye* ! The traditional oxymoron to describe the paradox of love here acquires a new force which tends to relativise its conventional use, for Emelye is his enemy not in causing the metaphorical death of the knight in love with her, but in being the occasion of Arcite's actual death in combat for her sake. Courtly values, as commonly understood, can be as effectively put in their place by this technique as was Chrétien's God of Love. This is not the occasion to rehearse the wide range of meanings of *triuwe* in Wolfram's *Parzival*, but I am convinced that the author depicts here his hero's slow progression from a courtly or feudal conception of the word, praiseworthy as far as it goes but certainly no absolute, to an unqualified acceptance of *triuwe* as love and compassion. Although there is no absolute antithesis between Parzival's initial and final understanding of this quality, we are made to realise that the feudal connotation is no more than a relative value and that it is precisely these feudal trappings that make it difficult for him to grasp the unqualified nature of *triuwe* as love. This is illustrated even more emphatically in *Sir Gawain and the Green Knight* in the case of the concept *cortaysie*. The English poet, well aware of his hero's reputation and skill as a lover, includes this as part of Gawain's courtesy and good breeding, but this makes the hero's position even more difficult in the temptation-scene where the lady of the castle can appeal to this reputation as a means to achieving her end. Gawain's situation would be considerably easier if his values had no place for courtesy and love, but as it is the contrast between two types of courtesy (for the lady this means little more than lust, suitably veiled) shows us the dangers to which Gawain's own values expose him, their two-edged quality.

On the stylistic level verbal irony can be employed against a topos of courtly literature and thus imply a critical dissent from received values. In the *Knight's Tale* Chaucer appears to be traditional in his recurrent references to a Maytime setting, but when at length we are told that this was also the setting for the fatal tournament (v. 1625 ff.) we have rightly come to be suspicious of such deceptive appearances. In this the English poet's attitude is close to Wolfram's, whose mocking dismissal of King Arthur in his stock Maytime setting is meant as a criticism of this Arthurian topos, utilised by Chrétien, but also as a form of self-irony, since Wolfram had himself earlier made use of the same convention. A comparable deflation of a recurrent topos is to be found in *Sir Gawain and the Green Knight*, where the hero's initial perfection is supported by a reference to Solomon as the patron of the pentangle, the emblem of Gawain's loyalty (v. 625 ff.), whilst this same Old Testament figure recurs later, after Gawain's imperfection has been established, as a type of fallen man's shortcomings (v. 2414 ff.). Both these views of Solomon are of course medieval commonplaces, but their combination, when applied to the hero, has the ironic effect of qualifying his ideal status and the literary convention that worked with this ideal status as an indispensable *donnée*. The stock expectations raised by the use of a topos can also be exploited ironically whenever the author of a romance uses a formulaic expression inherited from oral tradition to indicate his own distance from that tradition. For example, the formula *ine weiz* was earlier used as a straightforward statement of an author's ignorance or refusal to be tempted down irrelevant sidetracks, but when Gottfried feigns diplomatic ignorance after King Marke discovers the lovers asleep together in the orchard (v. 18214 : *ine weiz nach waz unmuoze*), this appearance of courtly tact also conceals a deeper irony at Marke's expense, so that the author is here tacitly inviting his audience into collusion against one of his characters. Wolfram, too, can use this formula ironically (but now at his listeners' expense) when he twice disclaims knowledge of the time when Parzival drew near to Trevrizent's cell (435, 5 ; 446, 3 ff.), but shortly afterwards has the hermit reckon out with painstaking accuracy the length of time for the knight's wanderings (460, 22 ff.). In sheltering behind this formula Wolfram is directing his irony against his audience (hinting at the contrast between the ignorance they share with Parzival and the author's control of the situation), whilst Gottfried's target was one of his own characters.

Some of these examples of verbal irony have suggested that their effect was not confined to their immediate context, but that, as with *triuwe* in *Parzival* or *cortaysie* in *Sir Gawain*, they could extend to a judgment of the whole work and of the courtly values it illustrated, whilst the last points have implied the possibility of an author consciously manipulating his audience's responses for ends which they cannot yet envisage. These two points provide a bridge to my second category (the irony of the narrator) and suggest that there is no clear break between the two categories : when verbal irony is no longer an occasional possibility, but a recurrent stratagem by which the author controls his effects, we have insensibly passed over into the irony of the narrator. I do not propose to discuss here whether we are correct to see the first distinction between poet and narrator (with all the ironic ambiguities which this shifting perspective renders possible) in the medieval romance, except to suggest that this distinction is only feasible once oral tradition has begun to yield to written composition, that this transition coincides with the emergence of the romance and that we must be ready to entertain the possibility of an ironic discrepancy between these two roles in the transitional genre of the romance.

Frequently, narrator's irony involves the adoption of a guise of innocent, fallible narrator (in the manner of Socrates), so that the view-point of the action which we are granted is a highly relative one. This is true of *Troilus and Criseyde* where the narrator is human enough to fall so obviously in love with Criseyde that we can no longer trust his objectivity, but it is even more fundamentally true of the *Canterbury Tales*. Here each tale is equipped with a fictional narrator (Chaucer even fictionalises himself so that he appears within his own framework to narrate, with captivating irony, the disastrously clumsy *Sir Thopas*), but the effect of this is to place each tale in a new perspective. The *Knight's Tale* is no longer Chaucer's story, but one told by the knight, so that we are invited to regard it as reflecting the knight and as subject to his limitations : a naïve innocence and a touching inability to see the tragic implications of the story which we, outside the world of the story as he is not, are able to perceive. The complexity of Chaucer's device (where the framework places us at a distance from the tales it contains) is unknown to the romance, but there are certainly parallels for his employment of the fallible narrator. Hartmann may not cast himself as the narrator of a German *Sir Thopas*, but he does go so far as to depict himself as a simple-minded, unsophisticated narrator in his encounter with Vrou Minne in *Iwein*. The occasion is the courtly commonplace of the exchange of lovers' hearts when Iwein departs from his wife, but when Vrou Minne claims that this is what happened Hartmann (who, like Chaucer, fictionalises himself as the narrator in this debate) replies as a simpleton, unable to comprehend how a body could live without its heart. That Hartmann depicts himself as stupidly ignorant of a courtly topos is said by Vrou Minne herself (v. 3011 : *Dô zêch mich vrou Minne, / ich wære kranker sinne*) who attributes it to his lack of experience in love (v. 3015 : *dich geruorte nie min meisterschaft*). The narrator eventually follows the version of events put forward by Vrou Minne, but not without resignedly stressing again his incomprehension (v. 3024 : *doch ergienc ez nâch ir rede hie. / ichn weiz ir zweier wehsel niht*). By doubly accentuating his distance from this exchange of hearts (inexperience and incomprehension) Hartmann has ironised a courtly topos whilst passing on to Vrou Minne final responsibility for an interpretation of love with which he feels no sympathy, but he has achieved this by the device of dissociating himself as narrator (clownishly present in this scene and meekly submissive to Minne) from himself as poet (in remote control of his audience's reactions to his parody of a threadbare convention).

Wolfram uses a similar device, to stress not his stupidity but his factual ignorance as narrator, in his encounter with Frou Aventiure at the start of Book IX, once his narrative has returned to Parzival's adventures. He employs this personification and dramatises his encounter with her as a means of explaining his ignorance of what had befallen his hero since he was lost to view, so that, by asking Frou Aventiure to give him news, he has opened up a gulf between himself as the poet with overall knowledge and the narrator, who needs to be given information by this fictional creation of the poet. By feigning ignorance as narrator (as he did with the *ine weiz* formula in connection with his hero's wanderings) Wolfram is also keeping his audience in the dark and thus indirectly strengthening the impression of the long lapse of time since Parzival occupied the foreground and the many adventures he must have encountered. Yet the control of his audience's reactions which Wolfram achieves by thus deliberately withholding information from them is paralleled by his appeal to his dubious source Kyot as a justification for keeping his audience at bay for so long. When Parzival first catches sight of Titurel in the Grail-castle Wolfram teasingly refuses to tell his listeners more at the moment (241, 1 : *Wer der selbe wœre, | des freischet her nâch mœre | . . . | her nâch sô des wirdet zît*), but later, when he grants them enlightenment, he claims that it was Kyot who instructed him to organise his narrative in this way (453, 1 : *Swer mich davon ê frâgte | unt drumbe mit mir bâgte, | ob ichs im niht sagte, | umprîs der dran bejagte. | mich batez helen Kyôt*). In doing this Kyot is simply recommending the same procedure which Wolfram elsewhere adopts as his own and which, at the start of Book IX, he excuses by sheltering behind a fictitious personification, so that the force of this parallel would suggest that Kyot, too, may be a creation of the poet with the function of justifying the narrator's teasing of his audience in ironically stressing, this time, the discrepancy between their knowledge and his. Yet the adoption of this kind of device (falling back on a non-existent authority, claimed as a source) is itself another form of narrator's irony, for the source Wolfram claims to be following (Kyot) is none other than the narrator at one remove, in other words the poet who has acquired the liberty to invent by dissociating himself from the narrator and by using the smokescreen of a fictitious source. This is precisely what Chaucer does when he refers to a non-existent author Lollius as his source for *Troilus and Criseyde* and to " olde stories " for the *Knight's Tale*. In both cases the actual source was Boccaccio (as was Chrétien for Wolfram), but the feigned source has the advantage that it cannot be checked, has the authority of antiquity and allows Chaucer to make his own alterations to the narrative.

A dissociation of poet from narrator is also implied whenever there are grounds for regarding one of the characters in the romance as a spokesman, however temporary, for the poet. In both the French and German versions of the Iwein story the figure of Kalogreant is imbued with the quality of self-irony which we have to attribute to Chrétien and Hartmann if they, as poets, are to stand aloof from themselves, as narrators. Some at least of this figure's self-irony must be conscious since, in narrating an adventure of his from the past, he is aware from the start of the ridiculous outcome and of the light in which he cannot fail to present himself. His very account in which the " hero " emerges as a shamefaced loser, flies in the face of the romance convention that the hero must be the victor and some of Kalogreant's remarks betray a self-awareness that amounts to a criticism of this convention. Admittedly, this opening account is meant also as a foil to Iwein's exploit when he successfully accomplishes what his predecessor had failed to achieve, but even this parallel between the two throws a dubious light on Iwein's success and, of course, the literary convention which is subjected to criticism by Kalogreant's burlesque account is one to which Iwein's adventure belongs (he is the hero and therefore must be the victor, although we are led to doubt the justice of this victory). By using this figure of Kalogreant as a mouthpiece Chrétien and Hartmann have been able to dissociate themselves from their conventional role as narrator and, from the vantage-point of a prehistory, to take up a critical distance from the values implicit in their main story. Ironically, they do this through a figure of gentle scorn, a buffoon knight who belongs to Arthur's court but, because of his break with convention, is not fully of it. As a partly ridiculous figure Kalogreant is similar to Hartmann in his conversation with Vrou Minne (where his literal-minded obtuseness gave him some of the licence of a court-fool, the privilege of belonging to the court whilst mocking its conventions), but there is a further parallel in the stock figure of Keie himself. Keie, as the senechal, is emphatically a member of Arthur's court, but as *der zuhtlôse Keiî* (*Iwein* 90) he constantly flouts its conventions. His criticisms may be rejected as evil-minded by those at whom they are aimed, but Keie always survives their resentment and his own humiliations to continue with his function of court-critic. His task is to put to the test, by voicing his doubts, the tacit assumptions of Arthurian society, to prompt an inspection of what would otherwise have still been taken for granted. His victims may reject his criticisms, but the poet often suggests that there may be a grain of truth even in his outrageous remarks and that the victim who shrugs him off too easily may thereby be condemning himself. In all these cases a narrative figure who can afford to ignore the conventions (the fictional Hartmann because of his incomprehension, Kalogreant because of his wry acknowledgement of knightly failure and Keie because of his privileged role as *der kâtspreche*) is the poet's instrument for questioning these conventions. Each character is a *persona* for the poet, allowing him the ironic freedom to dissociate himself from the narrator and, by means of this shift in perspective, to show values which might otherwise have remained unquestioned in a new light.

My third category, dramatic irony, rests on the contrast, unrealised by a character in the narrative but suggested to the audience, between the apparent meaning of that character's words or deeds and something else that takes place in the narrative. For its effects this type of irony depends on the superior knowledge of the audience, aware of a truth that the character cannot envisage, so that this category stands in its own ironic contrast with the irony of the narrator, where the responses of the audience are deliberately manipulated by a narrator who, by feigning ignorance or by means of a teasing secretiveness, withholds certain information from them. One type of irony therefore keeps the audience in ignorant suspense, as much in the dark as the character himself, whilst the other places them on a vantage-point of (temporary) omniscience and grants them an advantage over the character in the narrative. This shifting perspective, now appealing to our superiority and now undermining our certainty by reminding us of what we do not know, serves the purpose of relativising our convictions, thereby inducing in us a frame of mind complementary and receptive to the questioning of conventional values intended by the author in his dissociation of poet from narrator.

If we regard dramatic irony in its own right, however, and not simply its contrast with irony of the narrator, it is clear that a device which depends on the superior knowledge of the listeners can be successfully employed whenever the audience is already acquainted with a traditional theme (although this does not exclude the possibility that an author may hoodwink his listeners by deliberately disappointing their conservative expectations). For this reason dramatic irony may be encountered in epic literature, clerical or lay, where the traditional nature of the subject-matter is the guarantee that the audience will have that overall knowledge of events which the author of a novel theme cannot presuppose and which he must insinuate by indirect means, if he is to achieve any effects by dramatic irony. The author of the *Millstätter Exodus*, for example, could rely on knowledge of this biblical theme for his subject to carry its own irony when he came to describe at purposeful length the splendid knightly equipment of the Egyptian warriors in pursuit of the Hebrews (v. 3039 ff.) at a stage when, as his listeners well knew, all this was to be set at nought in the disaster of the Red Sea. Similarly, in the Alexander theme there is a latent ironic contrast between the overweening ambition and apparent success of this world-conqueror and what a Christian audience knew to be the facts, namely that he was an unwitting instrument in God's hands, the means by which imperial power was transferred to the Greeks as part of God's plans for the salvation of mankind. Here it is the providential framework of the story, knowledge of which any author could assume who chose such a theme, which affords an ironic commentary on events to a Christian audience, but elsewhere the framework may be more one of fatalism or determinism, as in Chaucer's *Troilus*, where the background presence of Fortune inevitably casts an ironic light on the lovers' happiness (for we are forewarned that it is soon to pass away) or on Troilus' enthusiastic praise of the god of love who is busy plotting his destruction. Our reception of foreground events is therefore qualified by what we also see of the background of fatalism, but even this background can then be relativised in its turn, as in *Troilus* again, where the hero, on dying, ascends through the heavenly spheres to enjoy the consolation of a proper perspective on human affairs, but, just when he seems to have joined his author at this remote vantage-point, the poet once more opens up the distance between them by leaving Troilus in his pagan heaven with the consolation of philosophy and escaping himself into a contemplation of the mysteries of Christianity.

The choice of a traditional or pagan theme must therefore have increased the occasions for making use of dramatic irony : knowledge of the literary tradition could be left to pay its own dividends, whilst a Christian audience could be relied on to play its own role in relativising the values of the pagan world (I think myself that the choice of such classical themes as Alexander and Aeneas at the start of courtly literature encouraged irony as a literary mode with far greater implications for the romance than in the epic works that preceded it). Yet the author who chose a traditional or pagan theme would not simply rely on it to achieve his effects for him, he would have to ensure by discreet hints that his audience would not miss the delightful incongruities of the life he was describing. If this is true of a well-known theme, how much more true must it be of those authors who, in turning to the *matière de Bretagne*, open up a new world of literary themes for Western Europe whose very novelty has the disadvantage, from the point of view of our problem, that these authors can no longer rely on knowledge of their theme to provide its own irony. Instead, they have to build into their narrative a number of well-chosen platforms which the listener is permitted to ascend and from which he, in contrast to the characters in the narrative, can enjoy a partial survey of the terrain ahead, before descending once more to accompany the still unwitting hero on his path through the narrative. From the point of view of the audience this results in a recurrent interplay between ignorance of the whole (which they share with the hero) and awareness (which they share with the poet) ; and a poet such as Wolfram or, even more skilfully, the author of *Sir Gawain and the Green Knight*, can achieve effects of great power by judging when to shift his listeners from ignorance to awareness or back again. These shifts can be straightforward, as when Wolfram gives us advance information about his hero in the prologue by describing him as *træclîche wîs* (4, 18). We therefore know that, however long it may take, Parzival will eventually attain to wisdom, whereas for the first part of the narrative the hero is not even aware of his lack of this quality (significantly, he first expresses such self-knowledge only after the instruction he receives from Gurnemanz). When he later fails to ask the question at the Grail-castle we are alerted to the importance of this omission by the narrator's passionate outburst (240, 3 : *Ôwê daz er niht vrâgte dô ! | des pin ich für in noch unvrô. | wan do erz enpfienc in sîne hant, | dô was er vrâgens mit ermant*), so that we are aware of the tragic implications of this scene at the time when it takes place before us. Yet we still have something to learn about this, for as yet we only know that there *are* tragic implications, whilst remaining ignorant as to how and why they should be so. Parzival learns about this (and we with him) only gradually, so that Wolfram forces upon us a simultaneous double vision : a wider view of events than his hero can enjoy, but also a narrow focus which ensures that our process of enlightenment parallels his. The latter is a guarantee that we shall feel with the stumbling hero and take his quest to heart as our own, whilst the former underlines the tragedy of human blindness to the meaning of events. In other words, Wolfram's irony remains compassionate, it avoids the easy irresponsibility which is the permanent danger of the ironist, that escape from mental paralysis at the cost of falling victim to moral paralysis. This is shown by a last example of his equipping the listener with the knowledge he requires to appreciate dramatic irony, for he not merely hints at his hero's tragic involvement (as at the Grail-castle), he also relieves the tension this creates. At the nadir of his career, when Parzival has been condemned by Cundrie, withdraws in shame from Arthur's circle and sets out in search of the Grail, the narrator consoles us by adding (333, 30 : *er was ouch ganerbe dar*). Yet even this assurance has its ironic ambiguity (which we may or may not realise at the time) for it says no more than that Parzival is destined by birth to come to the Grail (which we know already, since the narrative has shown us this), it does *not* necessarily mean that he is to merit the Grail-kingship by virtue of his behaviour there. We may not realise until later the risk we ran in assuming the best from this remark, but by then the danger is safely past and Parzival has proved himself.

A fourth category may be described as the irony of values. It has obvious connections both with verbal irony (where a parody of courtly vocabulary or clichés could reflect on the courtly ideals they stood for) and with irony of the narrator (whose double role as narrator and poet gives us a further view-point from which to question courtly conventions), but it is sufficiently important to be taken as a separate category. I shall confine myself to one example, the chivalric values of Arthur's court, and attempt to show how even this central ideal is not immune to an ironic scrutiny which the poet invites his listener to repeat for himself. When, in both the French and German versions of the Parzival story, the hero, known to Arthur only as victorious in so many encounters, is granted membership of the Round Table and welcomed with praise, we should realise that, in granting him such honours, Arthur's court knows only one aspect of Parzival's career : his success-story. It knows nothing of his failure at the Grail-castle. In other words, the Round Table knows only a flatteringly selective aspect of Parzival's career whereas we, who have witnessed more than has come to their attention, have a deeper knowledge of his character. Dramatic irony, when used to stress the discrepancy between our knowledge and Parzival's ignorance, will relativise the hero and show up his deficiencies, but in this instance, where it illustrates the difference between us and Arthur's court, it emphasises their shortcomings, their ignorance of the facts, and readiness, nonetheless, to grant Parzival the highest honours. Of course, even if the Round Table had known of Parzival's failure at the Grail-castle, this still does not mean that they would have refused admission to him for his failures elsewhere. However, their readiness to disregard this aspect, even after it has been brought to their notice by Cundrie, although betraying their warm sympathy with Parzival, still suggests that they have no interest in character, that membership of their circle might be granted to a knight far from perfect and that Parzival, in being struck to his core by Cundrie's reproaches, however little he may understand their justification, is demonstrating a profounder ethical sensibility than the court which hitherto, in our eyes as in his, had represented the highest criterion of chivalry. There is a double irony in this situation : at the moment when Parzival's public disgrace convinces him that he has been proved unworthy of the Round Table he behaves in a manner which suggests his inner worth, whilst the reaction of Arthur's court, however kindly meant, reveals that, ethically, it is of much coarser stuff.

This ironic reversal of roles (the Arthurian court which had previously acted as a supreme yardstick is surpassed by the hero at the moment of his public shame) is certainly not unique in Arthurian literature. In *Iwein*, for example, the Round Table plays a much less important part than in *Erec*, since Iwein, unlike Erec (at least in Chrétien's version), does not return at the end of his career to the Arthurian circle that was his starting-point. In the Parzival story the creation of a realm of the Grail to which no member of Arthur's court other than the hero is granted access further edges the Round Table from the centre of the narrative and casts a critical light on the absolute nature of the ideal for which it stands. But instead of taking these French and German parallels further, I should like to consider briefly an English episode from *Sir Gawain* where the priority of values is shown to be comparable with that in the Parzival scene. The English romance ironically disappoints our expectations by devoting itself to a hero, the paragon of Arthurian chivalry, who turns out to be, not larger than life, but all too human in his failure. There are other romances where Gawain may fail in his quest (with Wolfram he is unsuccessful in gaining access to the Grail-castle), but this is mitigated by the fact that Gawan is not after all the hero of Wolfram's work, so that his failure acts as a foil to Parzival's success. With *Sir Gawain*, however, the position is drastically different : he is the only hero, so that his failure strikes us with a force absent from *Parzival*, inviting us to consider whether, if even Gawain be flawed, any knight can attain to perfect chivalry. The irony of Gawain's position is that, at the end of the romance, he returns to Arthur's court and has to recount the tale of his adventures, culminating in his failure in the test. His position is disturbingly reminiscent of Kalogreant's at the beginning of *Iwein*, but appearances can no longer be saved by the English author as they were by his predecessors : with him Gawain's shortcoming is the centre of his work and no mere foil to his hero's subsequent success, his work closes on a note of imperfection, whilst Kalogreant's lack of success can be conveniently forgotten once Iwein dominates the stage. The outward token of Gawain's failure and lasting sense of shame is the belt which he wears and which had been the occasion of his fall. He takes all this seriously, his anguish in recounting his story is genuine and he wears the belt as a constant reminder of his imperfection. Arthur's court responds to this, however, on quite another level : they greet his account with laughter which, although it is kindly meant as consolation, strikes us as insensitive, jarring by contrast with Gawain's grief and refusing him the compliment of taking his feelings seriously. The moral coarseness betrayed by Arthur's court at this climax reminds us of the obtuseness which lurked behind their sympathy with Parzival after his disgrace, but whereas this impression was later lost to view in *Parzival* as we followed the hero ultimately to the Grail-castle and, like him, left Arthur's company behind us, the English author blocks this way out and leaves us with this view of Arthur as our last impression. Furthermore, there is unconscious irony in the fact that the court, to demonstrate its fellow-feeling with Gawain, should adopt the belt as its own token and wear it for the sake of Gawain. This is once more highly ambiguous, for if the belt has come to be a sign of the hero's imperfection, there is every justice in its being worn by the other knights of Arthur's court who cannot rival Gawain in eminence. But whereas he realises that this is so and has been convinced, by his adventure, of his human vulnerability, this insight is lost on the court because the adventure has of necessity not been theirs and because of their eagerness to make light of his sorrow. Gawain's failure in the test is therefore partly compensated by his sharpened moral awareness, but this is a gain which he has won at the cost of Arthur's court. The indefinable gap which separates him from his companions is an indication of the critical distance from which the Arthurian ideal can now be judged, even when it is not relativised by being measured against another authority such as the Grail-kingdom.

Imperceptibly we have already crossed over into my last category, that of structural irony, since we have been considering the ironic insights to be gained by contrasting, as the poet invites us to, the role of Arthur's court in *Parzival* with its function in *Erec* or *Iwein* and by noting the discrepancy between Gawain as the only hero of a romance and his function as a foil to the main figure. These examples suggest that ironic contrasts can be insinuated between one romance and another (the importance of Chrétien's *Cligès* as an *Anti-Tristan* is too well known to need any elaboration), but obviously these contrasts can also be built effectively into the one work. We find this not merely in the revolutionary grouping of different stories within a common framework (as in the *Canterbury Tales* where, for example, the *Knight's Tale* is ironically relativised by its successor, the *Miller's Tale*), but also within one single narrative. The technique of structural irony is commonly employed to juxtapose two figures in such a way that the discrepancy throws an ironic light on one. One of the results of the parallel quests of Parzival and Gawan is that the latter's social ease and chivalric renown highlight the hero's pathetic fumblings, while conversely Parzival's ultimate success at the Grail-castle, denied to Gawan, leads us to question even Arthurian renown. Erec's combat with Mabonagrin confronts us with a grotesque, but telling caricature of what Erec himself might so easily have become, Kalogreant's (and Iwein's) encounter with the wild man is used as an occasion for the poet to question their chivalric presuppositions, whilst the Parzival story goes a drastic step further : no longer does a knightly hero meet a wild man, but now the knight Karnahkarnanz meets a wild man, who is in fact the hero, Parzival, in the uncourtly wilderness of Soltane. These conjunctions of the hero with another figure who acts as a tacit comment on him are rich in implications for the way in which we are to judge the hero and the accepted values of knighthood, but I propose to consider instead another type of structural irony, more long-term in its organisation and more subtle in its effects : the meaningful discrepancy between two scenes, rather than two figures.

The two scenes I have in mind are Parzival's decisive appearance at the Grail-castle when he fails to ask the question and its structural analogue, Gawan's adventure at Schastel Marveile—my main point will be that in his Gawan episode Wolfram can afford to give us hints which are meant to illuminate Parzival's parallel experience, but which would be too obvious if placed in that scene. If we are to regard Gawan's adventure at Schastel Marveile as the crowning deed of an ideal Arthurian knight, two details must give us cause for wonder. A knight without his steed is like a fish out of water (as we know from Kalogreant's humiliating return *on foot* after his defeat), but when Gawan comes to the castle, ready for the supreme test he expects there, he is disconcertingly told to dismount and leave his horse at the gateway, so that we are already led to doubt how knightly the encounter is that awaits him. This is confirmed by the description of his adventure, for this takes place on a magical bed where Gawan is the humiliatingly passive target of a diabolic engine of destruction. There is a nice irony in the fact that Gawan, an erotic adventurer second to none, should have to undergo his climactic adventure in a bed, that this is where he should have to prove his knightly valour and not on horseback (567, 19 : *Sus reit er manegen poynder grôz*). This is highly suspect, for the other hero of a romance whose " adventures " take place in bed is the lover Tristan, whose leap from his bed to Isolde's Gottfried describes as a *poinder* (*Tristan*, 15187). Although Gawan's adventure is not an erotic one like Tristan's, it is clearly just as non-knightly. The purpose behind this scene is burlesque —to take Gawan, the flower of Arthurian chivalry, down a peg or two, to deflate his chivalry by placing him in a position where knighthood counts for nothing, but alongside this Wolfram has a serious aim—to prompt us to ask whether Parzival, in his analogous adventure, may not also be deliberately placed in a situation where his chivalric valour is irrelevant.

A faint allusion to Gawan's later predicament is given when Parzival comes to Gurnemanz' court and refuses to dismount, for in his inexperience he imagines that being on horseback is tantamount to being a knight. He is more amenable, however, when he comes to the Grail-castle : he dismounts before entering and even goes further than Gawan in being expressly stripped of all his knightly gear, but soon comes to regret this when reacting over-excitedly to an imagined provocation (229, 1 ff.). Even though Parzival reacts to what he finds here in a knightly way and regrets that he has laid aside his sword, the situation which confronts him is far from being that of a traditional knightly adventure, for what is in fact expected of him is a simple question of compassion of the ailing Amfortas. He fails to see the need for this and is so blinkered by knightly concepts that he still imagines that a knightly adventure was what was expected of him when, on the following day, he wakes thinking that his military assistance is urgently required by the Grail-king. He utterly fails to realise that something quite different from knighthood was wanted, that his trial was not military, but a moral test of compassion. Behind this lies Wolfram's criticism of the naïve optimism of knightly adventure, the belief that every case of suffering can be relieved by the knightly means of armed intervention—the poet doesn't reject this view (although he has his doubts about the homicide it involves), but stresses a truth unpalatable to chivalry, that it is nothing like an adequate answer to human suffering. Wolfram therefore relativises the concept of chivalric adventure by illustrating that compassion at large is of greater importance than the active compassion by means of armed assistance which is the hallmark of knighthood. In thus subordinating the knightly test of adventure to a higher form of moral trial the German author comes close to an English author two centuries later, for the hero's position in *Sir Gawain* is like Parzival's : he is prepared for a knightly test, the encounter with the Green Knight at the appointed time and place, but this blinds him (and for a time us) to the real moral test to which he is earlier exposed at Sir Bercilak's castle. Here at least it is fitting that Gawain's decisive test should take place in a bedchamber and that the verbal sparring he conducts with his temptress should have replaced the knightly jousting to which he was more accustomed when in search of adventure. The Ger-man and the English authors both conduct their heroes (and their listeners) to the unexpected recognition that their narrative, whilst illustrating the very real merits of chivalry, has also been at work in cutting its pretentions down to size by critically defining its limitations.

If one of the goals to which Parzival is led is a recognition of what *âventiure* really means (as opposed to what he thinks it means), then we might say that the verbal ambiguity of *âventiure*, like that of *triuwe*, has acquired a structural importance, that in this romance my first and narrow-est category, verbal irony, is related to my last and widest, structural irony. My argument has come full circle and although I have ignored some of the aesthetic consequences of irony (for example, its different functions and extent in oral poetry and written literature, its relationship to allegory or its contribution to a form of literary realism) I hope that the examples discussed have suggested something of the wealth and variety of ironic speech in the medieval romance and have shown that the masterpieces of this literature, so far from indulging in an adolescent idealisation of the chivalric world, are self-critical enough to afford us both aesthetic and intellectual delight. Cervantes, in ironising the conventions of the romance and in creating the novel as a form of anti-romance, made use of a literary weapon that had been forged by the medieval poets and which they had not hesitated to turn against themselves in the task of self-scrutiny. It is a fitting ironic conclusion to observe that the romance was enabled to live on creatively, even if indirectly, in the new *genre* that supplanted it.

D. H. GREEN

Cambridge

V

SOME OBSERVATIONS ON THE STATUS OF THE NARRATOR IN HARTMANN VON AUE'S *EREC* AND *IWEIN*

In both his romances, Hartmann the poet dramatises the process of telling in the figure of Hartmann the narrator, a speaker at times poring over the internal situation of the poem, at times turning away to present himself to the audience. There are, however, significant differences between *Erec* and *Iwein* in the narrator's attitude toward his tale and his audience. The many back references of the type *als ich iu gesaget hân* (453)[1] in *Erec*, which are not always necessary as reminders even in oral delivery, are not just signs of clumsy technique, but part of the narrator's general purpose in this work, which is to draw attention explicitly to his presence and to his procedures : repeatedly he tells us what he has said and what he is going to say, e.g. weaving into his list of the guests at Erec's wedding feast seven lines of the type " now I shall tell you " or " now I have told you " (1902, 1939, 1941, 1954, 2073, 2086, 2113). He tells us he is working from a source, but he also explicitly selects, for instance by saying (at times ironically) that he will be brief and tell only what is relevant (1446 ff., 2129 ff., 4299 ff., 5223 ff., 7429 ff., 7450 ff., 7476 ff., 7573 f., 7591 ff.). Thus we are recurrently made aware of the narrator's oratorical activity, and that we are hearing a tale that has been passed on to him, but in recounting which he makes his own decisions as to what is important, i.e. the narrator makes it clear that the audience depends on him for its view of the story, that the audience must trust him. And since he intimates a vast amount of background knowledge, ranging from information about Guivreiz (4299 ff.) to a familiarity with Lucan (5216 ff.), we accept him as a reliable authority.

The audience itself is frequently dramatised in *Erec*, for instance by the figure of *ratiocinatio*, as the narrator answers questions which the dramatised audience puts directly, or which the narrator anticipates (e.g. 5153 ff., 5386 ff., 6554 ff., 7106 ff., 7144 ff., 7207 ff., 7643 ff., 7680 ff., 8745 ff., 8775 ff., 9169 ff.)—a device which emphasises the narrator's authoritativeness and is characteristic of his eagerness to leap from the preterite tense in which he records the action into the present tense of interplay with his audience. Hartmann's " Erzählhaltung " in *Erec* is indeed " exceptionell publikums-unmittelbar ",[2] and nowhere is the narrator closer to his dramatised

---

[1] I quote from A. Leitzmann's ed. of Hartmann's *Erec*, Tübingen, 1957 (*ATB* 39) ; L. Wolff's ed. of *Iwein*, Berlin, 1968 ; M. Roques' ed. of Chrestien's *Erec*, Paris, 1955 (*Classiques français du moyen âge*) ; T. B. W. Reid's ed. of Foerster's text of *Yvain*, Manchester, 1942 (*French Classics*).

[2] G. Mecke, *Zwischenrede, Erzählerfigur und Erzählhaltung in Hartmanns von Aue " Erec "*, diss., Munich, 1965, p. 140.

audience than in the description of Enite's horse and saddle (7286-7766). Judged from the standpoint of an aesthetic which views the poem as an autonomous artefact whose every part should be functional to some purely internal system that leaves no place for a personal relationship between poet and public, this description would have to be regretted as tediously digressive. But interplay with an audience is part of the poet's aesthetic purpose in *Erec*.[3] The work has a clear social orientation in the light of which this passage is aesthetically legitimate precisely because the narrator is here less concerned to present a situation that is important for the internal action than to control the responses of his real audience by presenting his relationship with the dramatised, imagined audience as one of friendly interaction, with the narrator in dialogue with his audience, advising his friends to stay *hie heime* (7637) and accept his word, assuming the pose of *ein tumber kneht* (7480) but quickly showing his superior knowledge (7493-7525), ready later to reprove his audience by withholding information when the time is not yet, in his view, ripe for revelation (7826 ff.). Rarely in German literature before Hartmann can a narrator have assumed quite such explicit control over his material, and probably never before has the sheer process of telling assumed quite such an explicit status within the work, as a personal relationship between narrator and audience, as it does in *Erec*.

The narrator appears in a different light in *Iwein*. He is less ready than the narrator of *Erec* with explicit references to his oratorical and organising activities, he brings fewer formulae of the type " as I have said " and fewer reflections on his aesthetic procedures : he does not, for instance, parade his learning by telling us that he has much information which he is withholding for reasons of brevity, so that we are less often aware on reading *Iwein* than we are on reading *Erec* of the narrator as a man with a large store of knowledge that he could pour out if he had the time. In general, the narrator of *Iwein* uses the first person singular less often than does the narrator of *Erec*, and he addresses his audience less often explicitly in the second person : in the 10192 vv. of *Erec* (i.e. including the Wolfenbütteler Fragment) I count 142 occurrences of the narrator's first person singular (as pronoun alone or with a verb), whilst the 8165 vv. of *Iwein* have 71 occurrences ; in *Erec* the narrator addresses his audience in the second person on 125 occasions, in *Iwein* on 26 occasions ; and the first person plural is used in the narrator's voice (either as editorial we, or to embrace narrator and audience) 24 times in *Erec* as against nine times in *Iwein*. Statistics can lie, but these are telling figures. The audience is dramatised as speaking to the narrator only once in *Iwein* (7027 ff.), at least four times in *Erec* (7106, 7493 ff., 7826, 9169 f.) ; and whereas the narrator of *Erec* puts some thirty questions, many of which are really the audience's questions to which he supplies an answer (see above), the narrator of *Iwein* puts

[3] On the legitimacy, indeed necessity of the narrative poet's concern with his public, see W. C. Booth, *The Rhetoric of Fiction*, Chicago & London, 1961, pp. 89 ff. Booth's bibliography is an excellent guide to literature on narrators.

only eight questions to the audience in his own voice, of which seven are purely rhetorical questions closely linked to the action and not implying much audience participation (1262, 2416, 3735ff., 6867 ff., 6939 ff., 6980, 7279 ff.).[4] The public space[5] in which the narrator is in open interplay with a dramatised audience is indeed narrower in *Iwein*, and moreover the narrator of *Iwein* presents his story more scenically than the narrator of *Erec*, with less summary in his own voice : direct speech takes up a higher proportion of *Iwein* (52.7% of the work) than of *Erec* (31.4%)[6] and this contributes to the dominance of scene ; there are fewer descriptive passages in *Iwein* and these are more functional to the unfolding of plot and theme, and played less explicitly towards the audience than the descriptive passages of *Erec*, which are exploited strongly in terms of the relationship between narrator and audience ; and, as P. Salmon has remarked, the narrator's reporting of his characters' thoughts and feelings is more often backed up by visible gestures of the characters in *Iwein* than in *Erec*.[7]

It should be emphasised that these are differences of degree. Hartmann has not yet set about the task of eliminating the privileged narrator ! But our observations point already to a certain retreat of the " intrusive " personal narrator as we pass from *Erec* to *Iwein*. As a voice speaking in oral delivery, or imagined by a silent reader, the narrator is present throughout the works, but the narrator of *Iwein* is in less sustained rapport with a dramatised audience within the work than is the narrator of *Erec*,[8] and he asks us less often to take his word on trust, he appears to place us more directly before the actions, the words, even the thoughts of the characters, inviting us to form our own judgement : *daz mugent ir kiesen, ob ir welt* (*Iwein*, 2570). The narrator has become more questioning, less self-confident in his telling.

★   ★   ★

The shifts in the narrator's mode of presentation from *Erec* to *Iwein* are rich in implication for a purely stylistic approach to Hartmann's works : it may well be, for instance, that in working on *Iwein*, Hartmann was thinking

---

[4] The narrator's other question is an instance of *subjectio* (*Iwein* 3309 ; see P. Salmon, *The Works of Hartmann von Aue in the Light of Medieval Poetics*, typescript diss., London, 1956). Salmon brings a very useful account of the figures of words involving " the relationship between narrator and audience ", pp. 105 ff. ; and the decreased use of *ratiocinatio* and *subjectio* which he notes in *Iwein* by comparison with *Erec* (pp. 114 f. and 120) is, I think, characteristic of the most important difference which I am trying to point out between the two works in the narrator's attitude to his audience, for both· figures strongly imply a speaker in rapport with a hearer.

[5] I take the term from F. Goldin, *The Mirror of Narcissus in the Courtly Love Lyric*, N.Y., 1967, p. 122.

[6] See H. J. Gernentz, *Formen und Funktionen der direkten Reden und Redeszenen in der deutschen epischen Dichtung von 1150 bis 1200*, typescript diss., Rostock, 1958, p. 374 ; and Herta Zutt, " Die Rede bei Hartmann von Aue ", *DU* 14 (1962), H.6, 67-79. On scene and summary, see P. Lubbock, *The Craft of Fiction*, London, 1954 (first publ. 1921), pp. 68 ff., and W. C. Booth, op. cit., pp. 154 f.

[7] Op. cit., p. 306.

[8] See also H. Drube, *Hartmann und Chrétien*, Münster, 1931, p. 61, fn. 1 : " Im *Iwein* tritt die Gestalt des Hörers entschieden zurück . . .".

more in terms of written literature than he was with *Erec*, where his narrator is so conscious of speaking to an audience.[9] But in the context of the current debate on the *meine* of *Iwein*, the question of the narrator's status as ethical judge of the action has particular relevance, and it is chiefly to this question that the remainder of this paper will be devoted.

Predominantly in *Erec* one unambiguous ethical judgment is presented within the work as adequate to assess a given phase of the action, and on the main lines of the action the narrator guides our ethical sympathies firmly in his own voice. All the relevant characters, even the defeated Iders (1244 ff.), agree that Erec has acquitted himself well in his first combat, and the narrator places him clearly in his own voice as *der guote* (1056)—but he also forewarns us of the lovers' *verligen* by telling us of their intense desire to " spend a night or two together " (1857-1886). Erec's courtiers regret his *verligen* (2974 ff.), and the narrator records Erec's *wandelunge* (2984) in his own (the narrator's) voice with a firmness of judgement that does not allow us to consider a less critical interpretation of the hero's preoccupation with the marital bed : we are not allowed to contemplate the possibility of some moral nobility in the hero's abandonment of society for love, a possibility that Gottfried von Straßburg will present as a very real one when *his* lovers live *ane liute* (*Tristan*, 16849). Similarly in the *Joie de la curt* episode the narrator unambiguously approves Erec as *der guote* (9366) and places us against Mabonagrin (*sô mordic was sîn hant*, 9023 !), and even Mabonagrin welcomes his defeat as a release (9583 ff.), so that the conflict between his values and Erec's is perfectly resolved not by a compromise, but by Mabonagrin's accepting the values of Erec—and of the narrator. Conflicts between valid norms are only incidental in *Erec*, and when Enite has to choose between keeping her promise to her husband and saving his life, the narrator (e.g. by referring to her *triuwe*, 3143) leaves us in no doubt as to which is the superior obligation. On the important issues, everyone is in agreement in *Erec*, and when the work has been devised with such ethical clarity, the narrator's task as judge and guide is relatively simple.

Iwein is already, as it were, a romance of the second generation in which the new conventions are subject to more critical scrutiny, and *Iwein* has a greater diversity of ethical perspectives : a literary convention of Arthurian *âventiure* as the pursuit of personal *êre* clashes with the demands of social reality as Askalon (who condemns Kalogrenant as *triuwelôs*, 712) and Gawein (who has only praise for Iwein's success, 2879-2904) express radically differ-

[9] H. Linke, *Epische Strukturen in der Dichtung Hartmanns von Aue*, Munich, 1968, pp. 107 ff., contends that *Iwein* is more expertly constructed for oral delivery than *Erec*, and I do not maintain that *Iwein* would be a less effective work in oral delivery than *Erec*, but merely that it is arguably more effective than *Erec* if read silently, as written literature. Both Hartmann's romances combine elements of oral and written literature, but the robustness of outline in *Erec* and the narrator's constant references to himself as speaking point more towards oral consciousness in the poet, whilst *Iwein* has delicacies of style that are more evident if one reads the work at one sitting : e.g. the subtle echoing of earlier statements (5196-8 echoes 1548-56, 8139-48 echoes 2426-33) reveals to the reader who can refer back patterns that would be difficult to grasp in oral delivery.

ent views on the ethical legitimacy of unannounced provocations of the storm ; and Laudine is caught between the duty of respect for her dead husband and the duty to find a new protector quickly. Even the apparently sound new chivalric norm of proffering aid to those who ask is open to criticism when it leads to Gawain's defending an unjust cause ; in the resulting combat Iwein is placed (implicitly) between the demands of chivalric friendship which call on him to admit defeat (7561 ff.) and the obligation to fight on in defence of a just cause ; and the kingly virtue of adhering to vows causes some embarrassment when it leads to the abduction of Arthur's wife (4579 ff.). The course of events in *Iwein* indeed demonstrates just how inadequate some of the general ethical norms of courtly literature are as a guide to conduct in specific situations, and certainly *Iwein* is an ethically complex work in which actions are judged from more than one standpoint. The high incidence of direct speech and hence of scene rather than summary is, in part, a formal reflection of this ethical complexity as Kalogrenant, Askalon, Lunete, Gawein, Laudine, Iwein all give voice to norms and pass judgements in their words, all emerge as " disguised narrators " expressing fragments of the poet's whole truth :[10] even a figure of such minor consequence for the unfolding of plot as the woman who tells Iwein of a young knight's pursuit of *âventiure* (6320 ff.) can carry much weight as a spokesman for the poet's critique of chivalry. Already in *Erec*, of course, the narrator's commentary is by no means the poet's whole truth, for the poet does use his characters to impose his views, but as he passes judgement more often in *Iwein* than in *Erec* by the " indirect " means of his characters' words, so the narrator's commentary covers even less of the ground ; and whereas the narrator of *Erec* can rely on a central norm whereby to judge any one turn in the action, the narrator of *Iwein* is at times placed between a variety of voices not always in agreement and he not only covers less ground, but is also less consistently authoritative than is the narrator of *Erec* in judging the action ethically in direct commentary in his own voice. However, generalisation about the narrator's status as ethical judge is apt to merge into distortion when we consider *Iwein*, for his commentary varies in reliability and decisiveness from phase to phase in the unfolding of the action.

The narrator's ethical commentary in his own voice on Iwein's killing of Askalon and his sudden love for Laudine is remarkably scant and oblique. He refers in general terms to Iwein's *triuwe* (2427), but only after providing privileged inside views of his thoughts which place the hero in a critical light : the discrepancy between Iwein's public dismissal of Keii's taunts (856 ff.) and his private fear of just these taunts (1062 ff., 1530 ff.) seems

[10] W. C. Booth, op. cit., p. 152 : " In a sense, every speech, every gesture, narrates ; most works contain disguised narrators who are used to tell the audience what it needs to know, while seeming merely to act out their roles." This insight is more relevant to *Iwein* than to most works of the period, and it is a matter of no small consequence which of Hartmann's disguised narrators we follow. On dialogue as a means of orienting the reader, see also R. Koskimies, *Theorie des Romans*, Helsinki, 1935 (reprint Darmstadt, 1966), pp. 193 ff.

calculated to arouse critical detachment in the reader and to cast doubt on
the validity of Iwein's motives in attacking and killing Askalon. But the
judgement is only implicit. The narrator's much debated *âne zuht* (1056)
suggests more explicit disapproval, but the judgement is based on the
means of pursuit, whilst at the moment of the combat the narrator turns
away from the action and towards the audience with one of those technical
reflections frequent in *Erec* but rare in *Iwein*. Already in *Erec* the narrator
refused to describe a lady's *roc* on the pretext that he lacked an eye-witness
authority (8946 ff.), but that was a gratuitous piece of humour on a trivial
point. In *Iwein* the narrator's technical reflections carry more weight, and
his refusal to report the combat because of lack of an eye-witness authority
(1029-1044) is surely ethically motivated, is a means whereby the narrator
keeps himself and his audience distanced from the action at a point where
it is anything but exemplary. The device of diplomatic ignorance is here
used to avoid explicit condemnation of the hero.[11] With regard to Iwein's
love, the narrator praises his hero as a faithful host to *vrou Minne* (1585 ff.),
but since *vrou Minne* will later be characterised as less than ladylike when
she tells Hartmann to " shut his mouth " (3013) and since the narrator will
later refer to her as the cause of Iwein's degeneration to a naked fool (3249
ff.), such praise seems double-edged. Indeed, the narrator remains bemusedly
detached from the enslaved lover type throughout the work, and even
before his praise of Iwein the lover, he has taken pains to show how his
compassionate words contrast with the less noble thoughts of a man who,
because of his love, would not give *ein strô* if all Laudine's courtiers fell
dead (1432-1445). By such revelations of a discrepancy between appearance
and reality the narrator seems systematically to be undermining our faith
in Iwein, the knight and lover. But the criticism still remains implicit. The
reader has to supply the explicit judgement. And when the marriage between Iwein and Laudine is finalised, the narrator says that it was *michel
vuoge* (2417). Just when are we to take him seriously ? In what direction
is he guiding us ?

It is significant that he closes his account of the first phase of Iwein's
career, at another point of some ethical delicacy, with a further reflection
on the material of his delivery, the exchange with *vrou Minne* in which he
professes his failure to understand a literary commonplace (2995 ff.) and
maintains that he is speaking not out of personal opinion but at the command of *vrou Minne* (2984 ff.) and in dependence on his source (3025 ff.).
The narrator of *Erec* presents himself as one fully competent to understand
the main lines of the action, and when he shows his wisdom on matters of
love (e.g. 2364 ff., 3691 ff., 9169 ff.), we sense that the *poet* is speaking directly
to us. But the narrator's commentary in the early stages of *Iwein* (up to
v. 3028) is characterised by the recurrence of statements which cast doubt

[11] Illustrations of the device in A. T. Hatto, " *Ine weiz*. Diplomatic Ignorance on
the Part of Medieval German Poets ", in *German Studies presented to L. A. Willoughby*,
Oxford, 1952, pp. 98-102.

on his ability to understand the action, or which suggest that he is not convinced of the truth of what he is saying : he refuses to describe Iwein's combat because he "lacks an eye-witness" (1029 ff.), he says he cannot understand Laudine's and Iwein's exchange of hearts (2995 ff.), his qualifying *waenlich* of v. 2433 suggests doubt as to whether Iwein's and Laudine's married state is really so secure, he reports only as hearsay that the wounds of love last longer than those of sword and spear (1549 ff.) and says only "we are told" that a corpse will bleed in the presence of the killer (1355 ff.). Even when he comes out into the open with a firm *ich weiz* (1875), he "knows" only that women always change their minds out of *güete*, a clearly unreliable piece of knowledge which, if taken seriously, says more for his politeness than his acumen, and which will in any case be implicitly retracted when he describes a woman as *diu unguote* (5663) and tells how she changes *her* mind not because of *reht* and *güete* but under pressure of *gewalt* and *vorhte* (7704 ff.). Such apparent reliance on the views of others, however, such statements of doubt, limited understanding and bland politeness build up to a pattern which leads to our not accepting the narrator's every word as a direct statement of his own belief, still less as an expression of the poet's views.

Recent Chaucer criticism has shown that the medieval poet does not always identify with his narrator,[12] and a discrepancy between the views of the poet and the words of the narrator is especially clear in *Iwein* when the narrator professes in vv. 2995 ff. an ignorance that cannot possibly be shared by the poet. But elsewhere (e.g. when he develops the allegory of *minne* and *haz*, vv. 7041 ff.) the narrator shows a literary expertise that cannot

[12] The debate on the *Canterbury Tales* and *Troilus and Criseyde* can throw light on the problem of poet and narrator in other spheres of medieval literature, and I list some recent essays, with a few notes, so as to bring them into the German discussion : B. Kimpel, "The Narrator of the *Canterbury Tales*", *ELH* 20 (1953), 77-86 (Chaucer's comments show no awareness of a difference between poet and narrator) ; E. T. Donaldson, "Chaucer the Pilgrim", *PMLA* 69 (1954), 928-936 (Chaucer the pilgrim as a "fallible first person singular") ; M. W. Bloomfield, "Distance and Predestination in *Troilus and Criseyde*", *PMLA* 72 (1957), 14-26 (comments on the narrator's distance from his story) ; R. M. Jordan, "The Narrator in Chaucer's *Troilus*", *ELH* 25 (1958), 237-257 (Jordan comments on variations in the conspicuousness of the narrator and distinguishes sharply between the narrator's point of view and that of the poet) ; Rosemary Woolf, "Chaucer as a Satirist in the General Prologue to the *Canterbury Tales*", *Critical Quarterly* 1 (1959) 150-157 (an ironic tension between the poet's satire and the narrator's unjudging tone); Dorothy Bethurum, "Chaucer's Point of View as Narrator in the Love Poems", *PMLA* 74 (1959) 511-520 (the narrator is intensely involved in the action of *Troilus*!) ; J. M. Major, "The Personality of Chaucer the Pilgrim", *PMLA* 75 (1960), 160-2 (where Donaldson sees the narrator as credulous, Major suggests he reports with deliberate irony) ; G. D. Josipovici, "Fiction and Game in the *Canterbury Tales*", *Critical Quarterly* 7 (1965), 185-197 (Chaucer creates a narrator distinct from the poet with an irony that "seems Renaissance rather than medieval") ; R. A. Lanham, "Game, Play and High Seriousness in Chaucer's Poetry", *English Studies* 48 (1967), 1-24 (Chaucer remains detached from his narrator, who "falls in love with" Criseyde) ; H. Käsmann, "'I wolde excuse hire yit for routhe'. Chaucers Einstellung zu Criseyde", in *Chaucer und seine Zeit. Symposium für Wa. F. Schirmer*, Tübingen, 1968, pp. 97-122 (Chaucer was in too close a rapport with his public to dissociate himself distinctly from his narrator as a modern novelist can) ; D. Mehl, "Erscheiningsformen des Erzählers in Chaucer's *Canterbury Tales*", ibid., pp. 189-206 (the narrator of the *Tales* is not a psychologically sustained character).

easily be reconciled with his failure to understand a commonplace in vv. 2995 ff., and at this point two lines of interpretation are open to the reader. Either we take the narrator in *Iwein* as a consistently portrayed ironist who only pretends to be ignorant on occasion. Or (and this I find a more satisfying interpretation) he is not dramatised as a psychologically and intellectually thoroughly consistent persona, nor is his standpoint wholly and consistently separate from that of the implied poet ;[13] i.e. he is not a unified " character " like the persons within the action, he is not dramatised as consistently wise, foolish, or ironical. Hartmann's *Iwein* does not yet sustain the purist point of view admired by Lubbock, and I read the narrator in this work as speaking from various standpoints. Like Chaucer, Hartmann is, I think, still (even in *Iwein*) too much the court poet facing a present audience to detach himself constantly from and reflect consistently on his narrator, but at the same time Hartmann the poet does not constantly identify with his narrator, he has already discovered some of the advantages to be gained from a separation of poet and narrator : at times Hartmann the narrator is the implied poet speaking directly, at times he is a series of masks worn, or poses imaginatively assumed in the process of writing (and mimed in oral delivery) by the poet, at times he speaks wisely, at times he is distinctly limited in knowledge, and it is an important task of interpretation to assess just when the poet is speaking directly and when, and to what end, he is wearing a mask in *Iwein*. (The poet's oscillating between identification with and distance from his narrator is, I think, reflected in the fact that the narrator refers to Hartmann the poet in the third person in the prologue [*Iwein* 28, cf. *Gregorius* 171 ff. and *Der Arme Heinrich* 1 ff.], which might suggest that the poet thinks of the narrator as a separate person, but in the body of the text the narrator is also addressed as, precisely, Hartmann [*Erec* 7493, 9169 ; *Iwein* 2974, 2982, 7027], so that, if Hartmann the poet thinks of his narrator as a separate person in his prologues, he also forces a narrator in oral delivery to play the role, or roles, of *Hartmann* in the body of the text.)[14] This might seem a complicated way of reading a work often praised for its clarity, but recent opinion suggests that *Iwein* is not, after all, quite so simple a work ; moreover, what seems complicated to readers nurtured on later modes of narration may well have been self-evident to Hartmann's contemporaries.

However, whether we take the irony at any one point in *Iwein* as a product of the narrator's own ironic sensibility, or as lying in a discrepancy

[13] I take the term " implied poet " from W. C. Booth to indicate not the biographically real poet, but the " implicit picture " of the poet which forms in our minds as we read (op. cit., p. 151).

[14] Xenja v. Ertzdorff seems to differentiate between poet and narrator, but does not develop the point, " Spiel der Interpretation. Der Erzähler in Hartmanns *Iwein* ", in *Festgabe für F. Maurer*, Düsseldorf, 1968, pp. 135-157. Swantje Ehrentreich maintains that there is no trace of a " Rollenhaftigkeit des Erzählers " in Hartmann's works, and that " Verfasser-Ich " and " Erzähler-Ich " are " identisch ", *Erzählhaltung und Erzählerrolle Hartmanns von Aue und Thomas Manns dargestellt an ihren beiden Gregoriusdichtungen*, diss., Frankfurt, 1964, p. 352 ; G. Mecke argues the opposite case, op. cit., p. 6.

between Hartmann the wise poet and Hartmann the narrator who is dramatised for the immediate purpose as lacking knowledge, the important fact remains that this irony at times produces a disparity between the literal meaning of the narrator's comments and the views of the implied poet, and renders the narrator's commentary in the early stages of *Iwein* sufficiently ambiguous to provoke the opposed interpretations of those who see Iwein as still blameless when he marries Laudine and those who see him, with more justice, as already subject to the poet's criticism. Hartmann the poet is indeed dramatising Hartmann the narrator in this part of the work (up to v. 3028) in a variety of roles, now as a diplomatic ironist (1029-1044), now as an intellectually fallible first person singular who does not have complete control over and will not accept personal responsibility for the tale (2971-3028), and he is inviting us to think critically at those points where the narrator professes doubt, limited privilege, limited understanding : when the narrator says he cannot report on Iwein's combat because the hero was too *hövesch* (1040) to boast of his deeds, the poet is assuming a mask of politeness to launch ironic criticism by the device of an incongruously placed adjective,[15] and when Hartmann the narrator says he cannot understand the workings of *vrou Minne*, the poet is providing a burlesque criticism of that enslaving love which the narrator seems not to understand.[16]

Iwein's killing of a knight out of pure self-interest and his sudden, overpowering love for Laudine run against the values of Hartmann, the humane moralist. So much, I think, emerges from a reading of *Iwein*, without reference to Hartmann's other works. But the poet had ample reason to bring in the narrator's voice an ironic and to some extent ambiguous criticism. Firstly, by explicitly condemning Iwein in the narrator's voice as a murderer, he would have openly laid a charge against the hero so grave as to be capable of answer only in a work with the religious depth of a *Parzival*, whilst by keeping the criticism ironically oblique he reconciles it with the spirit of fantasy and comedy which largely determines the framework of the action in *Iwein*. (The aesthetic congruity of criticism by irony and burlesque is, perhaps, especially evident in the development of the love theme). Moreover, the very fact that all the characters involved quickly accommodate to the situation created by Askalon's death encourages the poet to keep his narrator's criticism oblique, for a basic stance of Hartmann as narrator in

[15] On the irony produced by " a disparity between the facts " (here Iwein's killing of a knight) and " the words chosen to represent them " (*hövesch* !), see P. Haidu, *Aesthetic Distance in Chrétien de Troyes : Irony and Comedy in " Cligès " and " Perceval "*, Geneva, 1968, pp. 44-46. Wa. Ohly, *Die heilsgeschichtliche Struktur der Epen Hartmanns von Aue*, diss., Berlin F.U., 1959, p. 108, sees " eine leise Ironie " in the narrator's defence of women, vv. 1873 ff. ; and the narrator's reference to Iwein's marriage as *michel vuoge* (2417) is interpreted ironically by Th. Cramer, " *Saelde und êre* in Hartmanns *Iwein* ", *Euph.* 60 (1966), p. 37.

[16] There is a double irony here in that the narrator appears intellectually fallible (and detached from the poet) by virtue of his failure to understand, so that we laugh at him, but his position is a common-sense one that causes us to align with him and against *vrou Minne* (see H. Milnes' brilliant, if at times over-stated essay " The Play of Opposites in *Iwein* ", *GLL* 14 (1960/1), 241-256).

his romances is his reluctance to criticise his central characters openly in his own voice when he lacks corroboration from reliable characters within the action. The narrator in Chrestien's romances comments less often than the dramatised Hartmann, but he is more willing to reveal the weaknesses of his heroes explicitly and on his own authority : for instance when Chrestien's Erec faces Guivret the narrator comments on his rashness (*Or fera Erec trop que fos, | se tost conuistre ne se fet*, 4968 f.), but Erec shows no awareness of having erred, whilst Hartmann reverses the situation, not even hinting at criticism in the narrator's voice, but bringing a speech in which Erec himself condemns his own *tumpheit* and *unmâze* (7007 ff.). Hartmann's sternest criticism is indeed brought preferably in direct speech, especially in the heroes' self-indictments (which are calculated to encourage self-criticism in the audience), whilst Hartmann the narrator tends to praise and justify his heroes in his own voice, is quick to assume the role of eulogist or defence counsel rather than impartial judge of his heroes in explicit commentary.[17] The resulting stance of politeness in narratorial commentary is perhaps even more sustained in *Iwein* than in *Erec* and is an important reason why we cannot accept the narrator's direct commentary in Hartmann's romances as necessarily the poet's most important truth, a truth which also includes the moral criticism of the heroes' self-indictments.[18] In criticising Erec's *verligen* the narrator does not need to abandon his stance of politeness, for he can simply agree with the reliable authority of Erec's court (and even here he strains at a gnat to praise Erec in vv. 2954 ff.), but since all the characters in *Iwein*, with the exception of the quickly forgotten Askalon, come to accept Iwein's killing of Askalon and his sudden love for Laudine, the narrator no longer has such an authority inside the action to lean on in open criticism, and distaste has to be registered in his commentary by a process in which criticism is implied by superficially polite words or protestations of ignorance. The irony of a disparity between the narrator's words and the poet's views in the early stages of *Iwein* is, in brief, the means whereby Hartmann the poet adjusts his humane idealism to an action part fantastic, part tragi-comical, and the means whereby he resolves the paradox of his position as both moral critic and polite eulogist

[17] This is as much a rhetorical stance on Hartmann's part as it is a personal desire to point to what is good in human nature : on the prescription of ample *laus* and sparing *vituperatio* in medieval literary theory see E. Faral, *Les arts poétiques du XIIe et du XIIIe siècle*, Paris, 1924, pp. 75 ff. and S. Sawicki, *Gottfried von Strassburg und die Poetik des Mittelalters*, Berlin, 1932, pp. 72 ff. The narrator's euologising does not, of course, extend to Keii, and it is one of the little ironies of *Iwein* that precisely Keii the mocker should express the narrator's dominant attitude toward his hero : " *ich prîs in swâ er rehte tuot, | und verswîge sîn laster : daz ist guot* " (2493 f.).

[18] W. Dittmann takes too narrow a view of Hartmann's procedures in *Iwein* when he writes : " Die zahlreichen Kommentare des Erzählers sind in der Weise ernst zu nehmen, daß *nur* unter ihrem Vorzeichen die Ereignisse gesehen werden müssen . . ." (" *Dune hâst niht wâr, Hartmann* ! Zum Begriff der Wahrheit in Hartmanns *Iwein* ", in *Festgabe für U. Pretzel*, Berlin, 1963, pp. 150-161 ; quote from p. 157 with my italics). K. Ruh has a sounder approach when he warns against reading the narrator's explicit commentary as Hartmann's whole truth, *Höfische Epik des deutschen Mittelalters. I : Von den Anfängen bis zu Hartmann von Aue*, Berlin, 1967, p. 108.

of his hero's behaviour. It is an irony that leaves us with far more inter-
pretative work to do than we have on reading *Erec*.[19]

Of the first 3028 vv. of *Iwein*, 1875 are in direct speech (or record thoughts
as if they were direct speech, e.g. 911 ff.) whilst only 1153 are in the narrator's
voice, and in these 1153 vv. the narrator addresses his audience explicitly
in the second person ten times (1031, 1045, 1107, 1135, 1361, 2565, 2570,
2582, 2716, 2989), throws out two rhetorical questions (1262, 2416) and
three times includes himself and his audience in the first person plural (50-56,
1355, 1586). The sequence of events from the account of Iwein's overstaying
his leave up to his return to Arthur's court (3029-6894) occupies 3866 vv.,
of which only 1686 are in direct speech (or record thoughts as if they were
direct speech) as against 2180 in the narrator's voice, but in this section,
although he says almost twice as much as he did earlier in his own voice,
the narrator addresses his audience explicitly in the second person only
seven times (3031, 3036, 3102, 3309, 3928, 4429, 5700), twice implicitly
addresses the audience by rhetorical question (3735 ff., 6867 ff.) and only
once links himself with his audience as *wir* (5969 f.). This shift towards
more summary in the narrator's voice and this fall in the number of times
he dramatises the audience by direct address are only crude statistical
reflections of a change in the narrator's attitude : he is, in this section, in
closer sympathy with and has firmer control over the human situation of
the poem. G. Mecke suggests that Hartmann's " Erzählhaltung " is more
" gegenstandsunmittelbar " in *Iwein* than in *Erec*.[20] But we need to distinguish between various kinds of distance in the relations of narrator,
reader (or audience) and action. The dominance of scene in the early stages
of *Iwein* brings the reader close in physical perception to the words and
gestures of the characters, but at the same time the narrator remains at a
distance by reminding us that the *âventiure* is of another's making (3025 ff.)
and by his protestations of doubt, limited understanding, etc. And the
irony of the narrator's commentary also keeps the reader at a certain critical,
ethical distance from the action. The particular manner of the narrator's
presentation in the early stages of *Iwein* thus brings us close to the action
in physical perception, but keeps us ethically distanced. In vv. 3029-6894
the narrator reminds the audience of the remoteness of the action in time,
e.g. by referring to a legal practice as obsolete (5429 ff.), and he remains
detached from Iwein's love in so far as it is an enervating, sense-robbing
force : he again reports the pain of love only as hearsay (5196 ff.) and humor-
ously expresses surprise that Laudine, carrying as she does Iwein's heart,
fails to recognise him (5456 ff.). But he is no longer detached from the
action in so sustained a manner as he was earlier, rather by comparing
Iwein's foreboding to his own experience he brings himself and his audience

---

[19] There is, of course, irony in the narrator's voice in *Erec*, e.g. the dramatised
audience tells him : " dû redest sam ez sî dîn spot " (7512) ; but the ironies are, I think,
incidental in *Erec* and do not systematically condition our response to the characters.

[20] Op. cit., p. 140.

close to the hero :

> im wîssagete sîn muot,
> als er mir selbem ofte tuot :
> ich siufte, sô ich vrô bin,
> mînen künftegen ungewin :
> sus nâhte im sîn leit.
> nû seht wâ dort her reit
> sîns wîbes bote, vrou Lûnete. . . .   (3097 ff.).

The *her* of v. 3102 places narrator and audience spatially with Iwein and, together with the psychological comparison, effectively concentrates the energy of the narrative by reducing our emotional distance from Iwein when he is about to be accused ; again at the end of the maiden's long search for Iwein the narrator brings himself and his public close to the action by comparing it to his own desired experience (5968 ff.). There are, in this section of *Iwein*, no technical reflections comparable with vv. 1029 ff. and 2971 ff. which placed the narrator (in different ways) at a considerable distance from the action. The brief references to a source (3052, 4861, 6456) do not suggest the narrator's doubt as to its veracity, and his earlier signs of lacking control over the action give place to a tone of greater authority as more of the action is recorded by summary in his own voice. The absence of technical reflections and the paucity of direct references to an audience make us less aware than we were earlier of being detached from the action, we are rather drawn into the human situation of the poem as the narrator records, for instance, the maiden's search for Iwein (5777-6012) and the meeting between Iwein and the maiden who would have tempted an angel (6471-6568) with a richness of mood and atmospheric detail that would be untypical of *Erec*, where the network of relations between narrator and audience in the public space of the work prevents the development of sustained " Stimmung " within the action.[21]

Iwein's ethical situation is presented with less ambiguity in the present section of the work than it was earlier. Criticism of Iwein has already been suggested in the narrator's commentary, and now Lunete brings an open accusation. Her reference to a disparity between Iwein's *wort* and his *muot* (3125 f.) brings as explicit condemnation that discrepancy between appearance and reality which has already provided implicit criticism in the narrator's voice, and her condemnation of Iwein as the cause of Laudine's *laster* and *leit* (3132, 3135) and as *triuwelôs* (3183) because of his failure to return and protect Laudine's *lant* (3158) echoes Askalon's indictment of Kalogrenant as *triuwelôs* because of the *lasterlîchez leit* of his provoking the storm (712 ff.)—an indictment which also reflected on Iwein.[22] Lunete is, indeed, a reliable spokesman for the poet's criticism of Iwein, she does not only accuse from the limited standpoint of herself and Laudine (from which

---

[21] See G. Mecke, loc. cit.

[22] The build-up to the accusation is also similar in both cases, cf. " *Mir nâhte laster unde leit. | nû seht wâ dort her reit | ein rîter . . .*" (693 ff.) and *sus nâhte im sîn leit. | nû seht wâ dort her reit | sîns wîbes bote . . .* (3101 ff.). These are more than chance parallels.

standpoint Iwein's transgression is trivial, a mere overstaying of his leave which he himself already regrets, vv. 3084 ff.) but, without knowing it, is part of the poet's broader strategy ; and the fact that a character inside the action launches so powerful an accusation when the narrator points at the same moment to the hero's *triuwe* (3089, 3210) is characteristic of the way in which Hartmann prefers to set about moral criticism of his main characters in *Iwein*. Having experienced the full weight of Lunete's charge, Iwein undergoes that pattern of symbolic death and regeneration which is central to all Hartmann's narrative works, and as he emerges as an exemplary character, demonstrating the *triuwe* of social responsibility and erotic fidelity, so the narrator, whose earlier praise was systematically qualified and turned to irony, can now place his hero without irony or ambiguity as *biderbe unde guot* (4860), *ein hövesch man* (6856), and his ethical commentary on the hero's adventures becomes more decisive and more acceptable, at face value, as the poet's truth than it was earlier.

Indeed, Hartmann's presentation of the hero's journey of chivalric penance suggests that the narrator's attitude towards tale and audience is ethically conditioned in *Iwein* in that he is least liable to deflect from a close reading of the internal situation of the poem, and draws his audience into closest emotive contact with the action precisely when the action is most clearly exemplary.[23] This tendency of the narrator is seen in reverse when Iwein returns to Arthur's court to face Gawein. Just as Iwein's killing of Askalon is judged from more than one standpoint in the work (he is *triuwelôs* if we judge from Askalon's angle, blameless according to Gawein), so the combat between Iwein and Gawein is open to more than one judgement : can we fully endorse Gawein's defence of an unjust cause ? but on the other hand can we really condemn him for (presumably) having trusted the elder sister ? Chivalric idealism presupposes trust in human relationships, and trust seems to have placed the flower of Arthurian chivalry in the wrong. A perspective opens up here which, if rigorously explored, would reveal the difficulty, indeed (given human nature) the impossibility of perfectly implementing in social reality the chivalric ideal of defending justice, for who is to say what is just ? Hartmann senses the problem when he has Iwein say that he will help anyone who asks *in good faith* (6003), which is certainly a sounder attitude than that of Gâwein, whose readiness to help all *vrouwen* (4275 ff.) seems dangerously uncritical. But the question of trust remains. What evidence does Iwein have that he is committing himself to a just cause ? Only the sweet words and the appearance of the messenger (6064 ff.). In this case, Iwein's trust is justified by events, but

[23] Put in a different way : the narrator brings his audience closest to the hero when he is most alone. In *Erec* the narrator still banters with the audience during the heroes' journeying (e.g. 4150 ff., 6669 ff.), but is in most sustained interplay with the audience when they enjoy Guivreiz' hospitality ; this suggests that the internal situation of the poem is already determining the narrator's relations with his audience to some, but only to a small extent. The narrator's responses are in general determined more by the internal situation of the poem in *Iwein* than in *Erec*, hence his closeness to Iwein, as a psychological response, and his lack of interplay with the audience when the hero is journeying alone and in crisis.

as the action of *Iwein* shows, words and appearances can deceive : Iwein, too, appeared trustworthy to Lunete (3119 ff.), and the knight who took Arthur's wife away seemed to be a man *der betelîchen biten kan* (4574). In his commentary on the combat the narrator does not explore the problem of trust raised by Gawein's position. It is not his wont to discuss ethical ambiguities openly. He simply registers distaste at the prospect of the possible death of a fine knight (6932 ff.) and follows up immediately with another refusal to dwell in detail on a combat (6939 ff. cf. 1029 ff.). For the only time in *Iwein* the audience is dramatised as speaking when the narrator interrupts his account of the first charge to exchange words with his audience (7015 ff.), then the combat is again interrupted as he develops a metaphor over 100 vv. (7125-7227) with a plethora of conceits and maxims that smacks of irony of overstatement.[24] Perhaps this rhetorical panache (which is more characteristic of the style of *Erec* than of the rest of *Iwein*) is intended partly to echo the military skill and sporting decorum of the combatants, but it is also part of the pattern initiated with the narrator's first direct address to his audience in vv. 1029 ff., it is a leap out of the action and into the public space of the poem motivated by the narrator's ethical distaste for the situation within the action.[25] But whereas the audience was kept at a distance from Iwein's first combat by the narrator's diplomatic ignorance, and from the workings of *vrou Minne* by the narrator's appearing as a simpleton, the narrator now keeps his audience distanced from the combat between friends by resolving it into formalistic aesthetic play.

Having turned away from a situation of some ambiguity, the narrator of *Iwein* never recovers quite the commitment to the action which he showed in his account of Iwein's deeds of *triuwe*. It is characteristic of the voices of agreement in *Erec* that the last word of direct speech is a universal " *âmen* " (9951), and typical of the narrator's control over the action that he ends with a full 170 vv. of summary in his own voice before his closing prayer (9954 ff.). There is no doubt in the narrator's voice as to his ability to judge his heroes' destiny, no questioning concern with emotional detail, but a decisively authoritative telling by which the narrator firmly circumscribes our response. He does not pretend to have invented the story, but he refers to his source with evident conviction that it is *diu wârheit* (10039), and if he does not lay claim to complete omniscience, he convinces us, by professing ignorance of the names of the guests at Erec's coronation feast (10061 ff.), that what he does not know is in any case hardly worth reporting.[26]

[24] Hartmann points the irony by placing these formally brilliant passages in the incongruous context of the narrator's expression of fear for the very lives of his knights (6932 ff.). On the importance of the " principle of contextuality " for the analysis of irony see P. Haidu, op. cit., p. 28.

[25] The narrator's clear expression of distaste in vv. 6932 ff. and the fact that he does not sustain interplay with the audience after the happy end to the combat suggest that his formal elaboration at this point is not simply a reflection of the sociable mood of Arthur's court.

[26] The points are always trivial when the narrator of *Erec* says he lacks information (e.g. 3497 f., 5172, 5657 f.), or when he puts some qualification on the truth of what he is saying (e.g. 185, 4283, 8201, 8698, 9209 f.).

The narrator has all the relevant information, information which allows him to place the heroes (as is the case in *Gregorius* and *Der Arme Heinrich*) finally in heaven, and not for a moment does he suggest in this robust final summary that there might be other evidence on the basis of which a conclusion might be reached that differs from his. The narrator of *Iwein*, by contrast, keeps up direct speech almost to the end, showing Iwein's and Laudine's reconciliation in a detailed scene of sentimental comedy that raises another ethical question : are we to believe Laudine, whose plea for forgiveness implies that she has incurred some guilt (8122 ff.), or Iwein, who says she is blameless (8133 ff.) ? Typically, the narrator leaves the matter open and hurries to the end with less than 30 vv. of summary. Even here he does not firmly direct our attitude toward his characters. His praise of marriage is couched in a long conditional sentence and qualified for the particular instance by the adverb *waenlich*, just as his earlier reference to Iwein's and Laudine's married bliss was conditional and qualified (8139-8148 cf. 2426-2433)—whereas the narrator of *Erec* was convinced of his heroes' progress (see *Erec*, 10119 ff.), the narrator of *Iwein* seems unsure, with this delightful self-quotation, whether much advance has taken place in Iwein's and Laudine's partnership. As the dramatised Hartmann closes (before his brief final prayer) with one of his familiar stances of limited knowledge, saying that he cannot report what happened later because his source runs out at this point (8160 ff.), we are left with the impression of a narrator who does not have full control over his heroes' destiny, who is detached from the human situation of the poem and who is unwilling to do more than surmise on his own authority. Such an open ending is uncharacteristic of the courtly romance as a genre and is, in the case of *Iwein*, more than a gratuitous rhetorical device.[27] Again, it is a question of distance. The narrator of *Erec* is convinced of the exemplary truth of his story and confident that he can " tell everything ", and if he rêmains constantly at some distance from the internal situation of the poem (though the distance varies), it is because of his sheer delight in interplay with his audience ; the narrator of *Iwein* takes less delight in such interplay, and if he remains always at some distance from the action (though the distance varies more sharply than it does in *Erec* from phase to phase in the work), it is because he is less confident than the narrator of *Erec* that he has all the relevant information, and also less convinced, when he comes to look back on the entire story, of its exemplary truth.

★   ★   ★

The *Nibelungenlied*, a late product of the heroic tradition, provides an apt point of contrast on which to close. The narrator of the *Nibelungenlied* never fills out even a single strophe with commentary in the first person

[27] That the open end, which is part of a meaningful pattern in *Iwein*, was not to every medieval reader's taste is indicated by the addition of less ambiguously happy ends in Mss. B. and *f* (See Th. Cramer's ed. of *Iwein*, Berlin, 1968, pp. 225 ff.).

singular, his ethical judgements are sparse and he tends frequently to include himself with his audience in the first person plural.[28] He appears as an anonymous transmitter of a traditional *maere* who does not regard his personal views as sufficiently important to be recorded at any length. The tale is everything, the teller of little consequence. Nor am I conscious of the mind of an individual poet manipulating this self-effacing, but very effective narrator for purposes of some deep irony. With the rise of the courtly romance, however, we can trace the emergence in German secular literature of individual minds no longer transmitting patterns with the continuity of spirit that links the *Nibelungenlied* (despite all the differences between epic and lay) with the *Hildebrandslied*, but reflecting critically on the material :[29] in Hartmann's romances, the narrator is named, he expresses personal views, he is already impelled by that " Reflektierenmüssen " which Lukács sees as characteristic of the novel,[30] and our relationship with the narrator becomes a larger and more complex part of our experience of the work. The courtly romance is less individualist, still more bound to a suprapersonal rhetoric than the tradition of the novel, but the narrator of *Iwein* is already a rather different figure from the narrator of *Erec*, and the narrators of Gottfried's *Tristan*, Wolfram's *Parzival*, Ulrich von Zatzikhoven's *Lanzelet* are yet different travelling companions guiding us along yet different lines : the narrator of *Lanzelet* often records his hero's doings with a moral *insouciance* that would trouble the dramatised Hartmann ; the narrator of Gottried's *Tristan* has neither the sustained, bantering humour of the narrator of *Erec*, nor does he ever appear as quite such a simpleton as the dramatised Hartmann in his conversation with *vrou Minne*, and he will penetrate more deeply than both into the psychology of his characters ; and (to point to only two features in so rich a poet as Wolfram), the dramatised Wolfram will strike up in *Parzival* a closer relationship with his hero than does Hartmann, and he will be a more explicit polemicist, far less committed to a rhetoric of politeness.

The dramatised Hartmann has a fairly consistent, though not strongly individualised personality in *Erec* : he displays his learning, he is a humorist, he has a fair grasp of moral problems. We cannot accept the narrator as simply the biographically real poet in Hartmann's works[31] (though it is easy

[28] See H. Linke, " Über den Erzähler im Nibelungenlied und seine künstlerische Funktion ", *GRM* N.F. 10 (1960), 370-385.

[29] On the poets' anonymity in Germanic heroic literature as the expression of a powerful sense of tradition, see O. Höfler, " Die Anonymität des Nibelungenliedes ", in *Zur Germanisch-Deutschen Heldensage*, ed. K. Hauck, Bad Homburg, 1961, pp. 330-392 (*Wege der Forschung* 14).

[30] *Die Theorie des Romans*, Berlin, 1963, p. 84 (first publ. 1916). In her sound defence of the narrator's voice, published at a time when dramatic modes were fashionable, Käte Friedemann categorises Hartmann, Gottfried and Wolfram as " naive Erzähler " (*Die Rolle des Erzählers in der Epik*, Berlin, 1910, reprint Darmstadt, 1965, p. 151) ; this judgement probably needs revision.

[31] E.g. in *Gregorius*, vv. 789 ff., Hartmann says he has never experienced *ungemach*, whilst in *Iwein*, vv. 3097 ff. he says he often has foreboding of his own *ungewin*. It is not likely that these rhetorical stances reflect a biographical development. See also L. Spitzer's methodological remarks in " Note on the poetic and the empirical ' I ' in

to take purism too far in distinguishing between narrator and biographically real poet[32]), but the biographically real Hartmann is probably of less interest to most readers than the implied poet. Even in *Erec* the narrator's explicit commentary does not cover the implied poet's whole truth, which is also recorded in symbol and direct speech, but if the narrator's commentary is less complex than the poet's whole truth in *Erec*, it nevertheless expresses the broad outlines of this truth : the implied poet's concern with the degrading and inspiring power of love is explicit in the narrator's commentary (e.g. 3691 ff., 9171 ff,), and the poet's control over the action is recorded when the narrator reminds us that we are returning to the main theme (1838 f.), refuses to tell something out of place (7826 ff.), and summarises so powerfully at the end. On the main points, I would contend, Hartmann the narrator is, in *Erec*, Hartmann the implied poet speaking directly to reader and audience. The narrator of *Iwein* is not only less liberal with the first person singular, he also presents a less consistent image. He speaks in many different roles : he is a courtier polite to women, but he also points to the guile of a woman ; he professes remarkable ignorance on love's psychology, but he also speaks at times as a literary expert and an experienced, much travelled man. It is certainly more difficult to assess the narrator's tone of voice in *Iwein* than it is in *Erec* (and even, perhaps, than in Gottfried's and Wolfram's works), and this difficulty has to be faced as an important one : when he says *des tôten ist vergezzen : | der lebende hât besezzen | beidiu sîn êre und sîn lant* (2435 ff.), is he making a neutral statement of fact, or directing irony against the one who killed and those who quickly forgot, or is he even, perhaps, reminding us, in a half-humorous way, that we are in a fictive world where " real " human emotions have to dance to the tune of the action ? There is no one simple and " correct " answer to this question of the narrator's tone of voice ; the dramatised Hartmann is, I think, sufficiently open to interpretation in *Iwein* for readers of different persuasions legitimately to make their peace with his voice in different ways at many points. The masks which come between the words of the narrator and the views of the implied poet are less easily penetrable in *Iwein* than in many other works of the period, the narrator is no longer such a simple dramatisation of the implied poet as he was in *Erec*, and the narrator's commentary contains less of the poet's whole truth : Lunete's indictment of Iwein is more drastic in tone than any accusation laid against Erec, whilst the dramatised Hartmann is, on the surface, perhaps even more.

medieval authors", *Traditio* 4, pp. 414-422, reprinted in L. Spitzer, *Romanische Literaturstudien* 1936-1956, Tübingen, 1959, pp. 100-112; and K. L. Schneider, "Die Selbstdarstellung des Dichters im Frauendienst Ulrichs von Lichtenstein. Bedeutung und Grenzen des Autobiographischen in der älteren deutschen Literatur ", in *Festgabe für U. Pretzel*, Berlin, 1963, pp. 216-222.

[32] See W. C. Booth, op. cit., pp. 364 ff., especially his account of Mary McCarthy's indignant reaction to the suggestion that she had reflected ironically on McCarthy the narrator in one of her stories : " I speak of myself in my own name, McCarthy " (ibid. p. 368). This statement of one author's intention to reveal "herself " does not, of course, solve the critical problem, but it is a timely warning against seeing distance and irony everywhere.

polite towards his hero in *Iwein* than in *Erec*, which suggests a larger disparity in *Iwein* than in *Erec* between the poet's full moral analysis and the narrator's explicit commentary; similarly there is a larger intellectual disparity between the position of the implied poet and the professed position of the narrator in *Iwein* than in *Erec*, as the poet's control over his characters' psychology and over the intricate development of plot contrasts with the narrator's protestations of limited knowledge and his reluctance to report on his own authority. Moreover, on the basis of extrinsic evidence, we know that when Hartmann the narrator says he can only report what has been told to him, he is not expressing the position of Hartmann the poet, who made many alterations of detail to Chrestien's *Yvain* and effected a large change in the indictment at Arthur's court. These discrepancies between the words of Hartmann the narrator and the whole truth of Hartmann the poet suggest the presence in *Iwein* of a large and complex strategy of the poet, only a small part of which is recorded in the direct commentary of Hartmann the narrator. The stylistic observations of the first part of this paper can here be placed in a broader context of values. By sending his first romance into the world with a narrator who tells of love and chivalry with such authority, Hartmann the poet is registering a clear vote of confidence in the new ideals, their comprehensibility, their relevance to the public whose responses he so firmly controls. In *Iwein* the poet presents, by ambivalent symbolic commentary (the wild herdsman, the fountain) and by his elaboration of detailed scene and dialogue, more evidence about human behaviour and human values than he did in *Erec*, he expresses judgements from more standpoints, he thinks more critically about love and chivalry, and by equipping his second romance with a narrator who assumes a variety of stances and whose commentary is thinner, less authoritative, more questioning than that of the dramatised Hartmann in *Erec*, he invites his public to form a more nuanced and a more independent judgment of the evidence than he did in *Erec*.

W. H. JACKSON

St Andrews

VI

THE PRESENT STUDY OF MALORY[1]

Until 1947 Malory's writings had been read fairly steadily for five hundred years, affecting at various times and in various ways, not all to be assessed, a variety of non-literary men and authors ; but almost totally neglected by critics. When Professor Eugene Vinaver brought out his famous edition in 1947 he could list only ninety-one books and articles on Malory. In his second, revised, edition of 1967 he listed one hundred and seventy-seven, and had missed some half dozen. No doubt his second edition will provoke much more work. The work of the last twenty years is greater than that of the preceding half millenium. The aim of the present essay is to give some account of what the past twenty years' work has produced. It is necessarily impressionistic and makes no attempt to duplicate bibliographical work already done elsewhere.[2] For this reason I shall concentrate upon topics and omit all but a few of many names of scholars whose work has been valuable.

The general situation must first be recalled, familiar as it will be to some readers. Malory's writing was first disseminated by Caxton's edition of 1485, of which only two copies remain (one imperfect) and a leaf of a third. The colophon names " Syr Thomas Maleore Knyght " as the author, asks for our prayers that God may send him good deliverance, and remarks that the book was finished in the ninth year of the reign of Edward IV, i.e. 1469-70. Caxton's edition is divided into twenty-one books of varying length and subdivided into some five hundred chapters. The chapter divisions are sometimes rather arbitrary, and there are also many descriptive headings (still a valuable guide through the enchanted forest but also occasionally off the mark), so it was always clear that Caxton had done some editing. His edition, as Benson has recently reminded us, was reprinted with some changes by Wynkyn de Worde in 1498, reprinted in 1557 and 1585 (twice); and was quite radically rehandled by Stansby in 1634 in an edition which held its own in successive reprints until the Everyman's Library edition, which was the first popular edition that went back to Caxton's full text, following the scholarly work of Sommer. Only since about 1900, therefore, has even Caxton's edition of Malory been at all widely available. But Caxton· was always the ultimate source of any version until the discovery in 1934 in the Fellows' Library of Winchester College, by Mr Walter Oakeshott

---

[1] This essay is the revised version of a lecture given to the British Arthurian Society at Gregynog Hall in September 1968. In revising I have been much helped by Benson's valuable article (see Bibliography) on a similar topic, and have inserted references to one or two other works that have come to my notice since the lecture was given, but the structure of the essay is essentially that of the lecture.

[2] For example, in the second edition of Vinaver's edition, *Works*, 1967. References to books and articles are made by authors' names, listed alphabetically in the Bibliography with details of their work.

while hunting for medieval book-bindings, of an almost complete manuscript of Malory's work, collateral with the manuscript Caxton must have worked from, but free from his editorial alterations. It is this manuscript, now called the Winchester Manuscript, that Professor E. Vinaver edited as *The Works of Sir Thomas Malory* in 1947, with an extensively revised second edition, 1967. The provocative title, with its assertion that Malory wrote not one book but eight quite separate books, has been not the least source of scholarly discussion since, as will be discussed more fully below.

Vinaver's editions have been widely reviewed, and this is no place for a detailed critique, but it may be useful briefly to describe some of the main characteristics of this major work of English scholarship in the twentieth century. The work of editing, so much more laborious and miscellaneous than criticism, and therefore often neglected in English studies, is shown here to be wonderfully fruitful and rewarding. One can quibble endlessly with Vinaver's text and commentary, but his level of accuracy is very high, and however much one may disagree, one is almost always standing on Vinaver's shoulders, if not on his corns. The enormous amount of varied detailed observation of Malory's text and meaning in Vinaver's edition is worth noting here because it is of the very essence of literary study, but difficult to sum up in a generalising essay. The edition also marks the end of the heroic age of Malory scholarship, from Caxton to now, when one man could hope to edit Malory's text. The greatness of Vinaver's achievement, as well as its inevitable and excusable shortcomings, show that in the future a major scholarly edition will only be possible with collaboration. Whether or not we have a plural *Works*, we shall certainly need plural editors.

The strength of Vinaver's commentary, and its principle concern, is the comparison between Malory's French originals (often themselves needing scholarly treatment before being available), and what Malory made of them. If Vinaver has sometimes missed or misinterpreted a passage or a reference (as the contributors to *Malory's Originality*, to be discussed later, have shown that he has) nevertheless he has reaped and led away the corn, and others coming after, gleaning here and there, may be full glad if they may find an ear of any goodly word. The weakness, if one may use so bold a word, of Vinaver's Commentary, is the lack of reference to contemporary or preceding English writing. This may lead to misinterpretation, but more usually simply to a blank, and we get very little help in understanding Malory's place in fifteenth-century English literature. Vinaver is in practice inclined to regard Malory's writing as self-generated, although as he himself says, " such a thought would be contrary to all we know of the history of prose ".

Vinaver's criticism is the twin of his scholarship. It must be said (perhaps especially by the present writer, who has sometimes disagreed with him) that Vinaver is the best critic of Malory we have. Penetrating shafts of criticism appear in the Commentary and are implied in many textual judgments ; some appeared in his general book, *Malory*, in 1929, but his best criticism is now chiefly to be found (with other matters) in appropriate places in the various Introductions in his edition. Any later edition produced by collaboration is unlikely to find so consistently high a level of lively, lucid, forceful prose. Its penetration, its wit, and not least those accurate lance thrusts and fierce passing slashes at other critics, as of a Lancelot come to judgment, proclaim him not only the devout disciple of Joseph Bédier, as he likes to describe himself, but in this as in other matters equal in rank with the master himself.

The criticism, like the scholarship, is the offspring of that fruitful comparison between Malory and his French sources ; and hence again Vinaver's unique strength and some weakness. What Malory has done has been lit with a bright light, but sometimes from an unfavourable and distorting angle. It is fascinating to notice how Vinaver has gradually, since 1929, become as it were used to Malory, and has come to think a great deal better of him—no small achievement by an author so intensively studied, and in itself a curious witness of Malory's still insufficiently accepted greatness. Vinaver's patronising tone in 1929 was modified in 1947, and still further abated twenty years after. But as in the Arthurian legend itself, earlier layers persist, and Vinaver still occasionally expresses a *parti pris* in favour of that French Arthurian romance which has not stood the test of time, and a contempt for Malory's English empiricism, interest in history, muddle, softness, moral concern, and bad French, in a work which still lives as literature. Vinaver can still contrast Malory's " prosaic context " unfavourably with the " poetry at its highest " of Chrestien, where surely the properly high valuation of Chrestien need not depress Malory's different currency.

In one respect Vinaver has a spot almost as blind in French as in English. His total lack of sympathy with the religious qualities of the legend of the Grail lead him to unsympathetic and consequently questionable judgments on the *Queste* both in French and English, and for correction we have to go to the work of Miss Tuve and to Moorman's chapter in *Malory's Originality*.

I now turn to discuss some of the main topics of the modern study of Malory.

One of the many paradoxes of the situation is that this " noble and joyous book ", as Caxton called it, has seemed to be written by a man whom modern scholarship has discovered to be, apparently, a complete scoundrel. Since Kittredge's work the opinion has been growing firmer that the author was the only Sir Thomas Malory apparently available, from Newbold Revel in Warwickshire. His date of birth is uncertain, but has been thought to be about 1393-4. Little is heard of him till about 1450, and then for ten years he has a lurid record of robbery, violence and rape. This outburst of youthful high spirits by a man in his late fifties and early sixties may be thought remarkable, but then of course the author of the *Morte Darthur* was *ipso facto* a remarkable man. Far from being burnt out by his excesses he endured imprisonment several times, broke out by climbing walls and swimming moats, and on one occasion repeated the violent crime of which he was later charged, went in an expeditionary force to war in the north in

1462, and finally concluded his book, full of years and very varied experience, if not of honour, at the ripe old age of seventy seven—surely the oldest medieval author, and rarely equalled since. He seems also at times to have been both Yorkist and Lancastrian. It is not only a book but a life that Hemingway himself might have envied. Such is the account, in outline, that has been accepted. But it was powerfully attacked by William Matthews in a book both learned and entertaining, *The Ill-Framed Knight*, 1966. He finds the traditional account impossible to accept as a life of our author because of Malory's age when he would have finished the book, and because of the dichotomy between a noble book and a villainous author. Matthews argues for a hitherto unknown Thomas Malory of Yorkshire as the author. Unfortunately, Matthews' book came out too late to be considered by Vinaver in his second edition. Vinaver nevertheless comments sceptically on Matthews' theory on the basis of an earlier paper read by Matthews. We know two things about our author for certain : that he was a knight, and that he was a prisoner. Neither of these is known to be the case with Matthews' candidate. Vinaver himself still follows the now traditonal view, but refers to forthcoming new evidence discovered by Dr Gweneth Whitteridge concerning pardons in the late 1460s mentioning Malory. Dr Whitteridge, it seems, will endeavour to prove that there were two Malory's, close neighbours, a political rebel from Newbold Revel and a felon from Fenny Newbold. This is somewhat similar an attempt to that of Matthews—to find an author who was not a villain. Vinaver himself does not attempt to distinguish between villain and mere rebel when listing the usual fairly comprehensive list of crimes alleged against Malory, and maintains in his second edition his former arguments, (*a*) that there is no connexion between an author's moral character and his works, and (*b*), (an otiose argument if (*a*) is true), that Malory's works are not so very moral anyway. He denies (quite unjustifiably in my view) that Malory's work reveals idealistic inspiration and moral and emotional refinement, and unconvincingly suggests he was chiefly interested in money. It must be added that Vinaver in his second edition has softened these aspersions and omitted the sentence in his first edition referring to Malory's " almost pathetic concern with material comforts ".

Purists, including Vinaver, may argue that the biographical problem has no relevance to what the book says, and there is some truth in this. But it is also true that any statement can only be fully understood in its total context, and the author's life is part of the context. An interest in literature leads naturally and properly to an interest in human lives, including the author's life, though " life " and literature are different things, and their relationships are multifarious and indirect.

The crux of the specific problem of Malory has not in my opinion been sufficiently examined : it is the question of Malory's date of birth. Matthews emphasises that it must be assumed to be 1393-4. The evidence is complicated and indirect. Vinaver in 1947 assumed that Malory would have been in his twenties when he inherited his family property in 1433 or 1434 suggesting a birth-date therefore of about 1410, but without evidence. In 1967 he omitted this speculation, but devoted a long footnote examining the puzzling Dugdale reference noted only in passing in 1947, which Matthews makes great play with in his own book. Vinaver also in 1967 notes without comment the record, emphasised by Matthews, that a Thomas Malory was in Beauchamp's retinue in Calais in 1414. If this Malory was our author he must then have been born at least by 1400, and probably earlier. Vinaver's account is now confused and unsatisfactory, but Matthews does not get us much further on, for if his assumed birth-date seems to make Malory improbably old as an author, I should have thought (perhaps I am innocent) that it also makes him improbably old for such a very energetic outburst of rape and violence as is attributed to him in his late fifties and his early sixties. Maybe some of the charges were false, but the prison-breaking, for example, would hardly be trumped up. If the birth-date goes, so does much of the rest of Matthews' case against the present assumption, though the problem of the Calais Malory remains. Perhaps our Malory *was* a robber, rapist, cattle-thief and turncoat, but (as C. S. Lewis once remarked) if all we knew of Tristram were charges prepared by King Mark's solicitors, would even he appear very different ? On the other hand, one cannot refute the case for Matthews' candidate, for the same reason that it cannot, so far, be proved ; namely, that there is no positive evidence.

Just as *The Morte Darthur* needs to be considered in the wider context provided by knowledge of the author, so the general effect and specific meaning of his work needs to be considered in the wider context of the general culture and general historical situation of the fifteenth century. Here Ferguson's excellent book stands alone. He shows how important *The Morte Darthur* is in contributing to the change (perhaps one of the most important in our social history) of the medieval knight into the sixteenth century gentleman with civic responsibilities. Ferguson perhaps under-estimates the extent to which this change was already under way in the late fourteenth century (consider, for example, the careers of some of the Lollard Knights associated with Chaucer) : and there may be other reservations to be made about his book ; but it is a most welcome improvement on the dismissal of Malory as merely nostalgic which is common to literary historians as diverse as the empirical Daiches, the Marxist Schlauch, and the Leavisite Speirs. (The only recent literary historian I have found who comes anywhere near understanding Malory, or even making use of Vinaver's now fundamental edition, let alone doing Malory some kind of justice, is the Italian Izzo. Of older literary historians Saintsbury has some splendid paragraphs.) It is unfortunate that we appear to have so few English historians who have any interest in literature, and who can use it and illuminate it as Marc Bloch, Georges Duby or F. J. Heer have done with their national literatures.

One of Matthews' most interesting pieces of evidence, and very well argued, is his examination of the language of the Winchester manuscript, which seems to be decidedly more Northern than would be expected, or perhaps would be possible, for a Warwickshire man. One must tread warily here. Attributions to dialect areas, especially in the later fifteenth century, are extremely difficult. Linguistic contamination by scribes during an unknown number of transcriptions is difficult to assess, especially as we have only one manuscript. Matthews' thesis will need much detailed philological testing in itself, and also comparison with other writings such as will be provided by the results of the labours on the dialect areas of Middle English texts by Professors Mackintosh and Samuels when they become available. At the moment, however, his case looks strong and most interesting. More work on Malory's language is needed. The outstanding contribution at the moment is the work of A. O. Sandved, though it is mainly limited to the verbs. Sandved also has some important criticisms of Vinaver's text. This work again will require much digestion, and deserves to be extended.

From consideration of language we naturally pass to style. Malory's has been much praised, often for quite the wrong things—its faded nostalgic beauty, for example—but it has until very recently been little examined. A full and satisfactory treatment of style depends on a firmer basis of linguistic knowledge and comparison than we yet possess. Nevertheless some interesting work is being done. The origin of Malory's style has been firmly and rightly attached to the vernacular chronicle that began to emerge in the fifteenth century, by Noguchi in an excellent article and by P. Field in a B.Litt. thesis. Such studies emphasise the simplicity and direct narrative bareness of his style, the lack of description, the simple but powerful moral and emotional response. The "popular" quality of his style is emphasised, as also by Simko, who perhaps has a Marxist axe to grind. All this is true enough, and it is particularly valuable that we are beginning to be able to place Malory in a satisfactory native tradition, not in any parochial way to deny or limit the French influence, but in order to establish how the French influence could be accepted and used. But I myself would also emphasise certain other characteristics of Malory's style, those qualities of dignity, emphasis, indeed magnificence, to be found especially in the last two sections, and especially in his dialogue, which, if I may be allowed to mention my own work, in the introduction to my edition I have called "ceremoniousness". My brief study of Malory's use of the second personal pronoun in the last two sections (Parts Seven and Eight) surprised me with the subtlety of its use. (It is unfortunate, but characteristic of the general neglect of Malory by scholars and critics, that Finkenstaedt's excellent study of " You and Thou " has nothing to say about Malory.) If we emphasise the colloquial directness of much of Malory's writings, we should not let modern prepossessions blind us to the fact that the gentry were just as well able to speak as the common people, and were a great deal more articulate. Nor should we let our sense of the nearness of the spoken word obscure the ceremonious courtesy and elaboration of what is said. Nor again should we forget that however close Malory and the chronicles are to the spoken

word, they are nevertheless *writing*. Professor McLuhan's fashionable dichotomy between " oral culture " and " print culture ", useful (if exaggerated)
as it is, requires the central term " manuscript culture ", already used by some
critics, which partakes of the elements of both the others. Malory's writing
is not that of a learned man, a cleric or a scholar, nor of a religious, nor of a
peasant (were it possible). He writes like a gentleman, secular, not moralistic
but pious, usually simple and direct, but courteous and when necessary
elaborate. One should also go further than this, first making a distinction
which is fundamental to the study of Malory, yet constantly overlooked.
Even though Vinaver's contention about the separate nature of the so-
called *Works* seems to me mistaken, it is nevertheless true that there is a
great variety in the achieved quality in *The Morte Darthur*. Leaving aside
that prose which is so heavily influenced by its alliterative source, the contrast between the fumbling beginnings of *The Morte Darthur* and the con-
summately artistic final sections is one that should constantly be emphasised. Malory both in his actual style and in his treatment of the story in
the beginning shows himself a beginner, and unluckily far too many readers
have been permanently put off Malory by the incompetencies of his first
stories. He is a beginner of genius and even in the first main section the
magnificent story of Balin and Balan reveals his power and depth, but
as a general rule Malory naturally enough gets better as he goes further
and clarifies to himself, and for us, (not necessarily conceptually) the
nature of his task and the effects he desires. We need to remember Malory's
progress and consequently uneven achievement when generalising about
his style. His purposes and interests changed, too. His handling of the
subtle distinctions between You and Thou, and of the concept of Honour,
for example, is clumsy and uncertain in the early books, brilliantly assured
in the last two main sections. So it is with his prose-style. And in the later
books that style seems to be highly mannered, musical, powerfully rhyth-
mical. Robert Graves in his idiosyncratic introduction to Baines's drab
reduction of *The Morte Darthur* accuses Malory of using rhetoric, and being
consequently less readable. There is a truth in the perception, if not in the
judgment, which scholars and critics have failed to recognise. There are a
few actual rhetorical devices, like the anaphora of Bors's lament for Launcelot, which do not make Malory's style in themselves " rhetorical ", but
they do point to its highly artistic quality. There are a few unquestionable
Biblical echoes, which one would imagine came chiefly through sermons, and
it is hard not to be reminded of fifteenth-century sermons in some of Malory's
more exalted and solemn passages. There may well be a biblical or liturgical
influence on Malory's prose, either direct or mediated through sermons.
Such topics and others await their students. We have no study of Malory's
stylistic relationship to French prose, and more remains to be done on his
relationship to English chronicle prose and alliterative verse. A sense of
Malory's internal chronological development should both help and be helped
by such studies.

The study of Malory's relationship to his French sources in terms of the re-handling of material has been the chief concern of both modern and older scholarship. Older scholarship, of which Jessie L. Weston's *From Ritual to Romance*, famous for other reasons, is an extravagant but not untypical example, was interested not in Malory but in following Arthurian legends back to pagan sources. It was to some extent part of a wider movement of the late nineteenth and early twentieth centuries that hungered in a curious way for " pagan mysteries ", and is evidenced by writers so diverse as Sir George Frazer, " Saki " (H. H. Munro), and Kenneth Grahame, as well as by Arthurian scholars. In more recent generations the interest has been more on the general historical development of a story or an idea, witness in this case to the modern interest in process rather than product. It is a perfectly proper and sensible interest but it subordinates *The Morte Darthur* as an autonomous work to other interests, e.g. the survival (or otherwise) of pagan Celtic themes. Since Malory is very late in this process the paradoxical result is that Malory, who wrote the only big Arthurian work of enduring *general* interest in Europe (this is not to say he wrote the best), may be treated as merely derivative and degenerate.

There has been much more work recently on Malory's relationship to his sources for the sake of his own work, studying his sources in order as it were to detach him from them. The outstanding example has been Vinaver's demonstration of how he disentangled the *entrelacement* of the French cyclic romances in order to produce a less interrupted development of a single strand of story. The team of scholars led by Professor Lumiansky has followed hot on Vinaver's heels, elaborating and correcting his findings in detail and sometimes questioning his conclusions as well as his main premise. The result has been an increased awareness of the autonomy and greatness of *The Morte Darthur* as a work of art in its own right, although Vinaver, as has already been suggested, while his admiration for Malory has increased with the years, retains a fruitful ambivalence towards his author. It is natural, therefore, that we have now a much sharper realisation of Malory's own contribution to this amazing corpus of legend.

There has, however, also been some advance in placing Malory within an *English* context not only of style but also of romance tradition. Matthews has emphasised his knowledge of the alliterative romances, and indeed his ability to write alliterative lines, and Benson has extended this to place Malory within the general literary tradition of English romance writing. There is probably still more to be done in this direction, which will improve our understanding of what Malory is about.

In contrast, however, to the points made by Benson, the general modern response to *The Morte Darthur* has tended to move, to sum it up in a phrase, from romance to realism. Older critics of the book, of whom C. S. Lewis may be cited as a late and eloquent example, particularly valued the element of mystery, of " faery ", the magic wonders ; it is " a rich feast of marvels, a tale ' of faerie damsels met in forest wide '." It is this indeed that our modern literary historians have been content to accept and despise. Vinaver hotly contested this view of Malory as long ago as 1929, though with characteristic subtlety. Any magic in *The Morte Darthur* is not Malory's but French, he maintained. He has continued to emphasise the prosaic and practical element in the *Morte*, not to Malory's advantage. Lewis well argued that if you take the magic seriously as a writer you do not multiply marvels, but this in a sense accepts Vinaver's perception of the prosaic, though valuing it for itself, and as a technique, quite differently. The problem is a complex one even if we remember the great variety of treatment, or at least, of success, within *The Morte Darthur*. The " whole book ", even if we accept it as such, is not so homogeneous as some critics imply.

Another, different, aspect of the problem is that the word *realism* is a very slippery one. The word is closely related to modern concepts of literature which are not directly applicable to older literature. Marvels can be presented realistically ; that is, by a literary technique of a kind to emphasise plausible appearances, plausible cause-and-effect, and Lewis loved this kind of effect in relating marvels, which is a little like serving ice-cream with hot chocolate sauce. This is the realism of romance, which does not deny the basically non-realistic structure. But realism is also closely associated with naturalism, which implies a scientific view of the world as a secular self-enclosed system, and of literature, or at least novels, as mirrors of that world, similarly organic and self-contained, available to inspection, comprehensibly, or at any rate, demonstrably articulated and motivated. Such a view is the very antithesis of romance, which insists on an inner or mental reality often at war with arbitrary appearances, and is supported by the extra-worldly, not scientific, laws of magic or religion. Miss Everett, in her well-known essay, showed very well how romance could use superficial realism, unconnected with naturalism, and Malory demonstrates this very well. On the other hand, the implication of Vinaver's work is that Malory was also working towards modern naturalistic realism, as may paradoxically be seen in the question of unity, to be discussed in a moment. But, again, when Vinaver talks about Malory's realism it often looks as if he means an inappropriate realistic treatment of romance material, sheer lack of imagination, failure to understand French finesse or even French grammar.

Malory is poised between romance-realism and modern naturalistic realism, and his special quality is complex, varying as it does from section to section. Field shows that Malory's French romance sources are often more realistic than he is in working out details of movements, etc. Indeed, anyone can see that Malory is not in the least interested in appearances. One of his great strengths, demonstrated from the first page onwards, is to seize on the heart of an action. His narrative is summary and in this sense analytic, or one might say revelatory, though not in a conceptual way : his dialogue is intensely dramatic. There is very little comment, though it does occur. He has a strong grasp of *reality*, however, even of physical reality, as can be seen for example in a comparison between his handling of the

ambush of Launcelot in the Queen's chamber and the much more naturalistic and detailed, but less convincing portrayal of the same episode by the
modern novelist T. H. White. Malory can give one a strong sense of reality
while employing very little realism, either modern or of the romance kind.
Nevertheless, in his post-Grail books he makes no essential demand on
supernatural forces, and these books in particular approach a modern
naturalistic pattern, as the stories of Arthur's birth and accession, of Merlin,
and of Balin and Balan, do not. Here Malory's relation to chronicle-history,
revealed in his style, and emphasised by Field and others, becomes interesting.
History in general has often a closer relation to romance than perhaps some
historians would have us believe, but the relationship is particularly close
and complex in Malory. There can be no doubt that he felt there was an
historical base, and an historical lesson for his countrymen, in his re-telling
of the Arthurian story. He might have denied he had done more than
invent dialogue (as Thucydides and Tacitus, unquestioned historians did),
or select from conflicting sources, as all historians do. It was not till the
seventeenth century that the Arthurian legend was expelled from sober
British and English historiography. Much of the sense of (literary) reality
in his treatment of Arthurian romance surely comes from Malory's own
semi-historical feeling for " reality ", besides his response to romance.

Various kinds of recognition of the " sense of reality " in Malory lie
behind that movement in modern criticism, from Vinaver onwards, including
Lumiansky and his colleagues, which has insisted on taking Malory seriously,
and which claims that what he writes is at its best great literature with real
living significance. The gain seems great, yet there is undoubtedly a loss in
the relative modern failure to respond to the " magic ", the " faery "; in a word,
to the true romance element. Our recognition of Malory's own contribution
to the Arthurian legends, of his own art, has paradoxically weakened our
perception of some of the things that are still there, in the very work of
art, *The Morte Darthur*, even if Malory himself did not invent them. Even
if Malory were as prosaic as he is claimed to be (which I do not believe) he
nevertheless translated, and often by his art enhanced, the very essence of
romance. He must have valued it or why undertake this huge task ?

Merely to praise Malory's " magic ", as the older critics were content to
do, would not now be of much use. In our intensely moralistic and naturalistic age we may lack the critical tools with which to examine it, though
Miss Tuve's book, which unfortunately only mentions Malory incidentally,
and Benson's analysis of the structure of *Sir Gareth*, offer suggestions, and
more could be evolved. (Northrop Frye's book on Shakespearian comedy
and romance also offers some valuable clues, as do Scholes and Kellogg on
" the nature of narrative "). Whatever the reason, along with discussion of
Malory's realism there has been a strong attempt, especially by Moorman
and Lumiansky, to see in Malory not only a writer with a strong moral
concern in the general sense, that is, an interest in human conduct, its
effects and values, but also a writer who is a moraliser, In his famous out-

burst " Lo ye all Englishmen " Malory does indeed moralise, but this is a rare case. Moorman claims that Malory wrote his book to illustrate failure in love, failure in chivalry, failure in religion. The united professors of America, in Lumiansky's collection, *Malory's Originality*, come down heavily on Launcelot's adultery. Lumiansky has posited the existence of a scene, which Malory did not get quite so far as actually to write, in which Arthur accuses Launcelot of adultery, and Launcelot repents and promises not to do it again. But of course he does, thus breaking his promise but accounting for the credulous Arthur's blindness to the goings-on which eventually Agravain forces him to notice, thus starting the specific train of events that leads to disaster.

One may well ask what has happened to Caxton's "noble and joyous book ". Both C. S. Lewis and Vinaver reject, for somewhat different reasons, this moralising Malory, and surely they are right. This is not to deny Malory's genuine moral earnestness ; we are not to think he has no values and views because he so rarely crams them down our throats. For the most part he allows us to draw our own conclusions, but also there is a great deal in *The Morte Darthur*, that vast miscellaneous and sometimes inconsistent (though not fragmented) romance, that cannot be pulled into the service of a design upon us. It is not a *roman à thèse*.

There has been some useful discussion of specific topics in which moral concepts must play an important part. Davies, Tucker and Moorman among others have usefully discussed love, chivalry and religion as they appear in *The Morte Darthur*. More of this would be welcome. Malory has his own independence within his dependence on others, and the disengagement of Malory's "originality" in this as in other respects has been one of the achievements of recent criticism. We now have a much clearer sense of the special quality of the book, its practicality and humaneness, moral concern, its gentlemanly yet pious secularism, and, for good and bad, a certain simplicity.

It may have been Malory's simplicity which led him to simplify the complex interwoven form of the French romances, thereby, as Vinaver has suggested, creating one of the earliest examples of modern fictional form, sometimes skipping hundreds of pages in his source in order to pursue a given story in a continuous line. He did not always succeed in mastering the problems or solving the inconsistencies (making least attempt, or being least successful, in the story of Tristan and of the Grail). He succeeded best in the last two main sections (parts seven and eight) following the story of the Grail. Vinaver is probably right in seeing this simplification as Malory's great contribution, the main source of his continuing appeal, as its demonstration is probably the great contribution and triumph of Vinaver's own studies.

The Winchester Manuscript, as is now well known, preserves some explicits, clearly authorial, which divide up the whole work into eight sections of uneven length, the story of Tristan being by far the longest.

The explicits clearly mark " natural breaks " and the first one asks those who will make any more of the Arthurian stories to seek other books. It was this odd request, the aptness of the breaks, and a number of inconsistencies between the various parts, that led Vinaver to the conclusion that the sections should be regarded as works as entirely separate as the various different novels of a modern novelist. This was surprisingly readily accepted by all reviewers except the learned and judicious R. H. Wilson of the University of Texas (who followed up the question in one of his many articles), probably because, as Benson shows, earlier readers, with some percipient exceptions like Bishop Hurd, usually considered the work to be an ill-digested heap of materials. In contrast to this acceptance there has since 1950 been a steadily increasing volume of dissent, of which the largest has come from the band led and conducted by Professor Lumiansky, finally concerted in the book entitled *Malory's Originality*. In this book the principal method of the various learned contributors has been for each one to take one of the separate main sections revealed by Vinaver and compare it with Malory's known or presumed sources and other closely related works. In so doing they have, at least to their own satisfaction if not Vinaver's, proved that the main sections are linked together, and have suggested many minor corrections of Vinaver's work, some of which he has accepted in his second edition, while he remains quite unshaken in his main assertion. Indeed, Vinaver has even modified the remark he made in 1947 that the last two sections " together form a coherent whole ", and has now deleted the remark in his earlier commentary that a certain passage is an attempt to link the *Queste* with the first section.

As I was one of the earliest to reject Vinaver's concept of eight entirely separate romances I must declare an interest here. I regret Vinaver's changes just mentioned because I think he was right in 1947, and I am as certain as I was in the article published in 1952 that the eight main sections are connected and designed to be read in sequence. To this extent (as well as in many useful minor details) Lumiansky and his colleagues are surely right, and indeed practically all modern scholars and critics of Malory would surely agree with them. Yet in the immediate controversy between Vinaver and Lumiansky (with others), if one had to agree with either side (which I do not) one's sympathies might well lie with Vinaver. His thesis seems to me unanswerable on the premises he assumes, and makes quite explicit, that unity depends on " organic " form, on a self-enclosed plot, coherent motivation, realistic and consistent presentation of character, thematic development, and over-all self-contained naturalistic consistency—the premises, in other words, of the usual criticism of the naturalistic novel. These are the premises, too, of Lumiansky and Moorman in particular, and the contestants are in this respect much closer than perhaps they realise, though Vinaver's notion of a nineteenth-century novel, being based on Proust, is a good deal more sophisticated than that of some of his opponents. In particular Moorman's attempt to construct detailed, coherent time-schemes, dominant themes of family feuds, and so on, though useful in making clear certain elements that are certainly in Malory and were not before so clearly recognised, must essentially fail. This is not how the book " works ", and Vinaver is quite right in seeing that it is not one nineteenth-century novel.

Vinaver seems on the other hand equally mistaken in his implicit assertion that it is *eight* nineteenth-century novels. If one looks at *The Morte Darthur* in terms of the tales it tells, there are about eighteen, for the most part as neatly finished off as the eight main sections (though without the *explicits*) and with about the same amount of interlocking. There is even some interweaving of tales within tales, especially in the story of Tristan (Section V). Even if we accept the eight principal sections they do not in their internal structure resemble modern novels. Olefsky has shown that even *within* Vinaver's divisions there are plenty of inconsistencies of the kind that Vinaver has maintained destroy the unity of the whole. If we are worried by such inconsistencies we must accept that *The Morte Darthur* is totally and disastrously fragmented. But Olefsky has also shown that Moorman's detailed unified chronology is equally untenable, although there is a broad chronological development in the book as a whole. We must accept that detailed naturalistic realism in chronological detail as in other matters of plot, motivation and characterisation is not to be sought, but that the broad coherence in these matters which is all that is required of romance can exist without such realism. We need more theoretical and practical explorations of such problems. The notions of what may constitute unity in various kinds of works of art have been little examined in relation to Malory. A. K. Moore has made a useful start, though he leans more to Vinaver's side of the argument than many might. R. K. Jordan's book on Chaucer, attacking the notion of " organic " form, though questionable in many respects and not mentioning Malory seems to be on the right lines and may offer some useful ideas which might well be applied to Malory. The detailed study of the form of *The Tale of Sir Gareth* by Benson admirably brings out how " odd " the form is if regarded in a novelistic light, but how effective if regarded as a romance, obeying the different laws of exposition of situation, revelation of identity, and analysis of moral situations through significant fantasy, which are characteristic of romance. In these questions of artistic forms we of the twentieth century have to beware of the totalitarianism and intolerance that threaten us artistically as well as politically. Modern dictatorship is utterly different from medieval kingship. In intellectual terms, too, we are tenderminded, in William James's terminology, seeking in our literature something like the inclusive generalisations of science, rejecting the variety, arbitrary " thisness ", and mystery of actual experience. Critics of medieval literature are, however, often old-fashioned, and it may be that if we were really responsive to the truly vital currents of our own time we should be encouraged to rely less on the rationalisations of what is essentially the late nineteenth-century novel, and turn **rather** to the apparently fragmented but differently ordered structures of some modern visual art and poetry. It may even be that the revolt against generalisation, rationality and planning of what is probably the passing modern fad of the " happening " can give encouragement to those who value medieval romance. We might recognise as one element of the contemporary social unrest that afflicts the best-regulated countries the expression of a natural and proper human hunger for the unregulated, the unique, the arbitrary, even for (significant word) the absurd. Perhaps medievalists may congratulate themselves on having recognised this genuine human need for the unconditioned long ago, and to have given it a satisfying and rational expression by reading Arthurian literature, that literature which above all admits of " happenings ", without sacrificing to them the sanity, decency, order, good sense, and rational generalisation, which are the foundations of good art as of good lives.

If this is so, the movement from romance to realism, valuable as it has been, must not run away with critical interest. Nor must our proper zeal to rationalise and codify our experience of *The Morte Darthur* be allowed to exclude that toughmindedness which accepts the arbitrary or unconditioned element in experience out of which true originality grows. We shall see *The Morte Darthur*, that is, as both history (of a kind) and romance ; we shall learn to understand its place in a complex European tradition, in a complex cultural context. We shall appreciate its necessary difference from the art and life of our own times, and so its capacity to enrich our own times as similarity could not. Out of all this will grow an ever-deepening sense of Malory's originality, and an increasing enjoyment of the range and greatness of his book.

D. S. BREWER

Cambridge

BIBLIOGRAPHY

Baines : K. Baines, *Sir Thomas Malory's Le Morte d'Arthur*, with introduction by Robert Graves, New York, 1962, Oxford, 1963.

Bennett : *Essays on Malory*, ed. J. A. W. Bennett, Oxford, 1963.

Benson : L. D. Benson, " Sir Thomas Malory's *Le Morte Darthur* " in *Critical Approaches to Six Major English Works*, ed. R. M. Lumiansky and Herschel Baker, Philadelphia, 1968.

Brewer : D. S. Brewer, " Form in the *Morte Darthur* " *Medium Aevum* XXI (1952), 14-24.

——(ed.) *Malory : The Morte Darthur, Parts Seven and Eight*, London, 1968.

Daiches : D. Daiches, *A Critical History of English Literature*, London, 1960, Vol. I.

Davies : R. T. Davies, " The Worshipful Way in Malory ", in *Patterns of Love and Courtesy, Essays in Memory of C. S. Lewis*, ed. J. Lawlor, London, 1966.

Field : P. F. Field (B.Litt. Thesis, Oxford, 1966).

Finkenstaedt : T. Finkenstaedt, " You and Thou : Studien zur Anrede im Englischen ", *Quellen und Forschungen zur Sprach—und Kulturgeschichte der Germanischen Volker*, N.F. 10, Berlin, 1963.

Ferguson : A. B. Ferguson, *The Indian Summer of English Chivalry*, Durham, North Carolina, 1960.

Izzo : C. Izzo, *Storia della Letteratura Inglese dalle Origini alla Restaurazione*, Milano, 1961.

Kellogg : See Scholes and Kellogg.

Kittredge : G. L. Kittredge, *Who was Sir Thomas Malory ?*, Boston, 1897.

Lewis : C. S. Lewis, Review of E. K. Chambers, *Sir Thomas Wyatt and some Collected Studies*, *Medium Aevum* III (1934), 238-9.

C. S. Lewis, " The English Prose *Morte* " in Bennett.

Lumiansky : R. M. Lumiansky, *Malory's Originality*, Baltimore, 1964.

Matthews : W. Matthews, *The Ill-framed Knight*, Berkeley, 1966.

McLuhan : M. McLuhan, *The Gutenberg Galaxy*, Toronto and London, 1962.

Moore : A. K. Moore, " Medieval English Literature and the Question of Unity ", *Modern Philology* 65 (1968), 285-300.

Moorman : C. Moorman, " ' The Tale of the Sankgreall ' : Human Frailty ", in Lumiansky.

—*The Book of Kyng Arthur*, Lexington, 1965.

Noguchi : S. Noguchi, " The Paradox of the Character of Malory's Language ", *Hiroshima Studies in English Language and Literature* XIII (1967), 115-134.

Olefsky : Ellyn Olefsky, " Chronology, Factual Consistency, and the Problem of Unity in Malory ", *Journal of English and Germanic Philology* LXVIII (1969), 57-73.

Sandved : A. O. Sandved, *Studies in the Language of Caxton's Malory and that of the Winchester Manuscript*, Norwegian Studies in English XV, Oslo and New York, 1968.

Saintsbury : G. Saintsbury, *A Short History of English Literature*, London and New York, 1898.

Schlauch : M. Schlauch, *English Medieval Literature and its Social Foundations*, Warsawa and London, 1956.

Scholes and Kellog : R. Scholes and R. Kellogg, *The Nature of Narrative*, New York, 1966.

Simko : J. Simko, *Word-Order in the Winchester Manuscript and in William Caxton's Edition of Sir Thomas Malory's " Morte Darthur " (1485) : A Comparison*, Halle, 1957.

Sommer : *Le Morte Darthur by Syr Thomas Malory, The Original Edition of William Caxton Now Reprinted and Edited by H. Oskar Sommer*, London, 1889-91.

Speirs : J. Speirs, " Survey of Medieval Verse (sic) " in *A Guide to English Literature*, ed. B. Ford, Vol. I, *The Age of Chaucer*, 1954.

Stansby : R. Stansby, *The Most Ancient and Famous History of the Renouned Prince Arthur King of Britaine*, 1634.

Tucker : P. E. Tucker, " Chivalry in the *Morte* " in Bennett.

Tuve : R. Tuve, *Allegorical Imagery*, Princeton, 1966.

Weston : J. L. Weston, *From Ritual to Romance*, Cambridge, 1920.

Wilson : R. H. Wilson, " How Many Books did Malory write ? ", *Texas Studies in English* XXX (1951), 1-23.

Vinaver : E. Vinaver, *Malory*, Oxford, 1929.

The Works of Sir Thomas Malory, ed. E. Vinaver, 3 vols. Oxford, 1947. (Second Edition), Oxford, 1967.

VII

THE TURK AND GAWAIN AS A SOURCE OF THOMAS OF ERCELDOUNE

Ingeborg Nixon, in an Edinburgh University Ph.D. thesis, listed the following elements common to *The Turk and Gawain* and *Thomas of Erceldoune* : the supernatural being, the subterranean journey, the command of silence, the castle, and the prohibition against food.[1] Comparison of the two works indicates, I think, that these correspondences are not random but resulted from the use of *The Turk and Gawain* as a source for the middle section of the narrative contained in Fytte I of *Thomas of Erceldoune*. Thomas' meeting with the lady, whom he sees come riding on a dapple-grey palfrey when he is lying under a tree, is not derived from *The Turk and Gawain*, but when the lady leads Thomas on his journey to the otherworld, it seems that suggestions for her part have been drawn from the turk, and for that of Thomas from Gawain. In one respect only the roles are reversed, for the lady, like Gawain, is on horseback, while Thomas, like the turk, is on foot.

Resemblances to *The Turk and Gawain* (*TG*) are confined to the area of *Thomas of Erceldoune* (*TE*) which is represented in the ballad *Thomas the Rhymer* (*TR*), and this suggests that *TE* is related to *TG* not directly but only through a work which served as a common source for *TE* and *TR*, and which may be called **TE/TR*. This relationship can be tabulated as follows :

Additional matter in *TE*, unrelated to *TG*, has obscured the closeness of the parallelism between *TG* and those parts of *TE* which have equivalents in *TR*. Here, comparison is made between *TG* and the relevant sections of *TE* which have such equivalents and so may be considered representative of **TE/TR*. The narrative discussed runs consecutively in the ballad.[2]

---

[1] " Thomas of Erceldoune " (1947), pp. 11-12 and 16-17. I am grateful to Dr Nixon for allowing me to quote from her thesis. The similarity between the two otherworld journeys is also noted by David C. Fowler in *A literary history of the popular ballad*, Durham, N. C., 1968, pp. 139-40.

[2] *TE* is quoted from the Thornton MS. text in *Thomas of Erceldoune*, ed. James A. H. Murray (E.E.T.S.), O.S. 61, London, 1875, but Murray's square brackets are omitted. Six variants of *TR* are printed in F. J. Child's *English and Scottish Popular Ballads*, Boston & New York, 1882-98, reprinted Dover Publications, New York, 1965 : *A*, *B* and *C* at I.323-6, and *D*, *E* and *Tam Lin M* stanzas 4-12 at IV.454-5 and 458. The section of the narrative under discussion can be found in *B* 5-12 and *E* 7-16, plus *Tam Lin M* 9.

The sole text of *TG* is unfortunately in the part of the Percy Folio where halves of the pages have been destroyed.[3] The romance opens with the arrival of the turk, a dwarf, who asks if any there will " giue a buffett & take another " (ll. 1-36). Half a page is then missing, but apparently Gawain strikes the turk and is then bound to accompany him until he is prepared to return the blow. It is the following two sections that seem to have provided source material for *TE/TR*. The turk and Gawain journey for more than two days and then enter a hill (ll. 37-74). [Half a page missing.] They arrive at a castle where there is a feast set out, but Gawain may not eat or drink anything except what is provided by the turk (ll. 75-112).

Most of the passages in the section at ll. 37-74 which do not contain direct references to the buffets or Arthur's court seem to have been drawn upon for the journey in the Thomas narrative. There is, first, an exchange of words before the entry into the hill. In *TG*, this is opened by the turk :

> " And yett I shall make thee 3ise as feard
> as euer was man on middlearth,
> > this court againe ere thou see."
> Then said Gawaine, " my truth I plight,
> I dare goe with thee full right,
> > & neuer from thee flye."   (39-44)

In *TE*, the order is reversed, Thomas giving his promise before the lady speaks :

> " Here my trouthe j will the plyghte,
> Whethir þou will in heuene or helle."
> Scho sayd, " Thomas, take leue at sonne & Mone,
> And als at lefe þat grewes on tree ;
> This twelmoneth sall þou with me gone,
> And Medill-erthe sall þou none see."   (107-8, 157-60)

The need for courage, brought out overtly by the turk's threatening language, is implicit in the stanza spoken by the lady. The word " middlearth / Medill-erthe " occurs in *TG* and *TE*, and in both texts the word " see " comes at the close of the expression of the idea that the mortal will not return to what is familiar to him for some time. Gawain and Thomas pledge themselves to accompany their guides in similar words, " my truth I plight / my trouthe j will the plyghte".

Secondly, there is the actual entry, when the turk leads Gawain and the lady leads Thomas into the interior of a hill. In each case the word " Merke / myrke " is used of the darkness :

> He led Sir Gawaine to a hill soe plaine ;
> the earth opened & closed againe,
> > then Gawaine was adread ;
> the Merke was comen & the light is gone ;
> thundering, lightning, snow & raine,
> > therof enough they had.   (*TG* 66-71)

[3] BM Additional MS. 27879, pp. 38-46. *TG* is quoted from *Bishop Percy's Folio Manuscript*, ed. John W. Hales and Frederick J. Furnivall, London, 1867-8, I.88-102.

> Scho ledde hym jn at Eldone hill,
> Vndir-nethe a derne lee ;
> Whare it was dirke als mydnyght myrke,
> And euer þe water till his knee. (*TE* 169-72)

Both Gawain and Thomas are brought to the point of speaking woefully of their suffering :

> Then spake Sir Gawaine & sighed sore,
> " such wether saw I neur afore
> in noe stead where I haue beene stood." (*TG* 72-4)

> The montenans of dayes three,
> He herd bot swoghynge of þe flode ;
> At þe laste, he sayde, " full wa es mee !
> Almaste j dye, for fawte of fode." (*TE* 173-6)

A journey for days on end which causes the hero to suffer severely from hunger comes at this point in *TE* but before the entry into the hill in *TG* :

> they rode northwards 2 dayes and more ;
> by then Sir Gawaine hungred sore,
> of meate & drinke he had great need. (51-3)

The presentation of food follows the statement of hunger in the narrative of *TE*. The lady leads Thomas to a garden where there is plentiful fruit, but warns him against it :

> Scho lede hym in-till a faire herbere,
> Whare frwte was growand gret plentee ; . . .
> He pressede to pulle frowyte with his hande,
> Als mane for fude þat was nere faynt ;
> Scho sayd, " Thomas ! þou late þame stande,
> Or ells þe fende the will atteynt." (177-8, 185-8)

The reference to " þe fende " relates this garden to the Christian earthly paradise, but the prohibition against plucking the fruit is clearly connected with the taboo on eating the food of the otherworld. Thomas is tempted by the fruit as Gawain is tempted by the feast set out in the empty castle in the third section of *TG* :

> A Bord was spred within that place,
> all manner of meates & drinkes there was
> for groomes that might it againe :
> Sir Gawaine wold haue fallen to that fare,
> the turke bad him leaue for care ;
> then waxt he vnfaine. (83-8)

Both Gawain and Thomas are on the point of eating when they are forbidden by their guides. After this, in *TG* :

> the turke went forth, & tarryed nought ;
> Meate & drinke he forth brought,
> was seemly for to see. (98-100)

He invites Gawain to eat, and Gawain does so, and drinks " ale, & after, wine " (l. 107). G. L. Kittredge noted as a point of comparison with *Thomas the Rhymer* that " the Turk will not let Gawain touch any of the viands set forth in the underground castle, but brings in safe victual for him ".[4] The

4 Child, op. cit., II.505.

offer of alternative safe food and drink occurs in the ballad after the prohibition against plucking the fruit :

> " But I have a loaf and a soup o wine,
> And ye shall go and dine wi me." (B 9.1-2)

The incident does not occur in TE, which seems to have omitted this element in the narrative of the common source.[5]

The lady now shows Thomas ways to heaven and hell, but the Christian otherworld material in TE has no counterpart in the extant portion of TG. She then points out a castle :

> " Seese þou ȝitt ȝone faire castelle,
> þat standis ouer ȝone heghe hill ?
> Of towne & towre, it beris þe belle ;
> In erthe es none lyke it vn-till." (217-20)

Similar lines occur in a later section of TG, where the turk shows Gawain the castle of the giant King of Man :

> he lett him see a castle faire,
> such a one he neuer saw yare,
> noe wher in noe country. (125-7)

The next stanza of TE which has a ballad equivalent contains a much more distinctive idea :

> " When þou commes to ȝone castelle gaye,
> I pray þe curtase mane to bee ;
> And whate so any mane to þe saye,
> Luke þou answere none bott mee." (225-8)

This idea seems to be present also in the fragmentary ending of the stanza with which the third section of TG opens :

> ". . . . . . made them noe answere
> but only vnto mee." (75-6)

Ingeborg Nixon comments that " when the story resumes, the turk is apparently telling Gawain to speak to no one but him, in almost the same words as Thomas' lady "[6].

In TE, a journey to the castle and entry into it follow the warning to Thomas :

> Vn-to þe castelle scho tuke þe waye.
> In-to þe haulle sothely scho went ;
> Thomas foloued at hir hande. (252-4)

Similarly, in TG :

> To the Castle they then yode :
> Sir Gawaine light beside his steed,
> for horsse the turke had none ;
> there they found chamber, bower, & hall,
> richly rayled about with pale,
> seemly to look vppon. (77-82)

The use of the definite article at the first appearance of the castle in the text of TG (l. 77) indicates that the castle had already been introduced in

---

[5] This point is discussed in my " Comment on the Rhyme-Scheme of Two Stanzas in Thomas of Erceldoune ", Notes and Queries, N.S. 16 (1969), p. 48.

[6] Op. cit., p. 11. The word " made " at l. 75 is not fully legible in the manuscript and may be open to question.

the preceding lost half-page, and it may be that the lady's pointing out of a castle in *TE/TR reflects this earlier reference rather than, or as well as, the reference to the castle of the King of Man mentioned above. This element is included in italics in the following comparative outlines of the two other-world journeys.

(1) Gawain gives his promise to accompany the turk, and (2) they journey for more than two days, Gawain on horseback and the turk on foot, and Gawain becomes very hungry. (3) They enter into darkness through a hillside. [Half a page missing. ? *They see a castle.*] (4) Gawain is not to speak to anyone but the turk, and (5) they enter the castle. (6) Here there is a feast set out but the turk forbids Gawain to eat. The turk then brings other provisions and Gawain satisfies his hunger and thirst.

(1) Thomas gives his promise to accompany the lady, and (3) they enter into darkness through a hillside. (2) They journey for three days, the lady on horseback and Thomas on foot, and Thomas becomes very hungry. (6) The lady leads Thomas to a garden where there is abundance of fruit, but forbids him to eat. She then provides food and drink for him. *The lady points out a castle.* (4) She instructs Thomas not to speak to anyone but her when he arrives there, and (5) they enter the castle.

The Thomas narrative follows the same order as TG with the exception of (2) which comes later, and (6) which comes earlier, so that the mention of extreme hunger is followed directly by the temptation to eat. If TG was the source, the different order in *TE/TR can probably be accounted for, at least in part, by the desire to tighten the structure of the narrative.

The similarities in words and in sequence of narrative and conversation between TG and TE, and the occurrence in both texts of an unusual combination of motifs, seem to me to suggest not just the independent use of a common stock of otherworld material but specific indebtedness. If the relationship proposed in this article is accepted, *The Turk and Gawain* can be dated in the fourteenth century, before Chaucer's *Sir Thopas* which made some use of *Thomas of Erceldoune*.[7]

E. B. LYLE
Edinburgh

---

[7] Laura H. Loomis, " The Tale of Sir Thopas " in *Sources and Analogues of Chaucer's* " *Canterbury Tales* ", ed. W. F. Bryan and Germaine Dempster, Chicago, 1941, pp. 488 and 524.